Commodities for
Every Portfolio

Commodities for Every Portfolio

How You Can Profit from the Long-Term Commodity Boom

Emanuel Balarie

John Wiley & Sons, Inc.

Published by John Wiley & Sons, Inc., Hoboken, New Jersey.
Published simultaneously in Canada.

Wiley Bicentennial Logo: Richard J. Pacifico

For general information on our other products and services or for technical support, please contact our Customer Care Department within the United States at (800) 762-2974, outside the United States at (317) 572-3993 or fax (317) 572-4002.

Wiley also publishes its books in a variety of electronic formats. Some content that appears in print may not be available in electronic formats. For more information about Wiley products, visit our Web site at www.wiley.com.

Library of Congress Cataloging-in-Publication Data

Balarie, Emanuel, 1979–
    Commodities for every portfolio : how you can profit from the long-term commodity boom / Emanuel Balarie.
        p. cm.
    Includes bibliographical references and index.
    ISBN 978-0-470-11250-2 (cloth)
    1. Commodity futures.   2. Portfolio management.   I. Title.
    HG6046.B324 2007
    332.64′4—dc22   2007008877

Printed in the United States of America

10 9 8 7 6 5 4 3 2 1

To my wife, Kelly. This book would not have been possible without your unwavering love, thoughtful insight, and support. You are truly the coauthor of this book.

Contents

Preface

I t is no secret that commodities have been on a tear of late. On one end of the spectrum, agricultural commodities have roared to new highs, and on the other end, metal prices and energy prices have rallied off their most recent lows. Even commodity markets that have struggled over the last year have quickly turned around in the midst of increased demand from the same old players, China, India, and other developing economies. To put things into perspective, Chinese imports of copper picked up a staggering 44 percent in January 2007 after many analysts prematurely predicted a slowdown in Chinese copper demand.

Indeed, there seems to be no end in sight to this commodity boom. Demand continues to be robust and supply constraints continue to be of concern. Of course, the increased need for raw materials by China and other developed economies (as well as the continued need for these same materials by developing economies) is a sizable reason for this continued demand growth. This demand has become so intense that many countries are looking at securing the vital natural resources that are needed for economic survival.

In 2005, for instance, China National Offshore Oil Corporation made a bid to purchase Unocal Oil. While this bid did not go through

(Unocal eventually merged with Chevron), it did reaffirm China's emergence on the global commodity scene. In early 2007, China's two largest steel companies—Baosteel Group and Wuhan Iron & Steel Group—made it known that they were interested in investing in Australia's iron ore projects.

This continual appetite for commodities not only underscores the current supply and demand imbalance facing the commodity markets, but it also brings to light the rapid growth that is taking place in other parts of the world. In fact, few people realize that China is one of the fastest-growing markets for luxury cars. BMW, Jaguar, Bentley, and Rolls-Royce all experienced significant gains over the last several years in terms of cars sold. When it comes to substantial wealth, more than 300,000 Chinese already have a net worth of greater than $1 million.

While this undoubtedly represents only a minute segment of the population, it speaks volumes for the growth and wealth creation that has occurred in China over the last few years. In other words, China is no longer the agrarian society of yesteryear.

Yet while all of these occurrences point to how far industrializing economies have come in terms of growth, and their subsequent impact on commodity consumption, it is still only the beginning of a multiyear transformation. Similarly, we are still in the early stages of this long-term commodity boom.

Purpose of This Book

Because we are still in the early stages of this commodity boom, writing this book could not be timelier. My goal is to have something for everyone . . . or at least for every portfolio. Whether you are an experienced commodity trader or simply looking for a better understanding of the commodity markets, I am confident that this book will provide you with insightful information and convincing reasons as to why you should participate in the commodity boom. I also believe that this book will present you with the basis for why commodities, as an asset class, have a place in every portfolio. Last, this book will also provide you with several different ways to participate in this commodity boom.

Interestingly enough, when I was first approached about writing this book, I struggled with the direction and focus. I knew that I wanted to write about this commodity bull market that I have so adamantly proclaimed over the last several years, but I was wondering who my target audience would be and what I wanted them to take away from the book. I quickly realized that many investors lack a basic understanding about the commodity markets. That is, they might know about the commodity markets in a general sense, but they don't really know how the commodity market functions and what factors are instrumental in determining futures prices. If they did, they would have participated several years ago.

I also found out that this lack of understanding is often compounded by the fact that many people have a misconception about commodities. Because of misconceptions, many investors have shied away from the commodity markets, despite some prolific gains in these markets. For this reason, it was important for me to write a book that provides the foundation for how commodity markets work, why they are so integral to our daily lives, and how commodities can not only provide investors with an opportunity to profit but also balance out their portfolios with an undervalued and underrepresented asset class.

How This Book Is Organized

As a result, it was quite clear that I had to focus on establishing the case for commodities from the ground up. While some of the content will be basic for more experienced commodity investors, it is necessary and fundamental for the new commodity investors. Indeed, investors who simply want to learn more about the commodity markets in an easy-to-understand way will find this book even more rewarding.

Part One, "Understanding the Commodity Markets," addresses these questions:

Are we in a bull market or a bubble?

How are commodities and inflation correlated?

Which significant factors contribute to both rising and falling commodity prices?

How do the futures markets work?

What is the purpose of the commodity futures markets?

What are the common myths associated with commodity markets?

What role do commodities have in the modern portfolio?

Besides wanting to write a book that describes the commodity markets clearly, I also wanted to provide a backdrop for the different ways of participating in these markets. I realize that many investors have different portfolio goals and want to tap into this long-term commodity boom. In Part Two, "Participating in the Commodity Markets," I look at the various investment vehicles that readers can use to participate. Specifically, I answer these questions:

Should I invest in futures, stocks, mutual funds, or exchange-traded funds?

What are the different types of commodity mutual funds?

What should I look for when selecting commodity producing companies?

What are differences among companies that profit from rising commodity prices?

Last, I wanted to outline some different ways in which readers could take the next step and actually profit from this commodity bull market. Given the fact that everyone has a different investment portfolio, I answered some questions that might help readers select which type of strategies to implement. Part Three, "Strategies to Profit from the Commodity Markets," looks at:

What types of strategies work best in this environment?

What are the advantages of having a managed approach to the commodity markets?

Why does gold have such an important role in the commodity portfolio?

What are some additional sources (third-party assistance) that can help during the different stages of this bull market?

What makes this book even more relevant now is that we are still in the early stages of a generational bull market in commodities. Taking the time to learn about these markets and the advantages that they offer today can better help you position your portfolio to profit from the moves that will occur in the future. And by the time you finish reading this book, I hope you will have a firm understanding of why we are in the midst of a multiyear bull market and why commodities should be an integral part of every portfolio. This knowledge will help you make the leap from understanding the current bull market to actually participating in it.

Acknowledgments

Writing this book was truly a team effort. Throughout the writing process, many people along the way have provided support, guidance, and simple encouragement. Words alone cannot begin to express my sincere gratitude for these individuals.

I am thankful for my parents, John and Maria Balarie, who sacrificed so much so that I would be able to achieve and accomplish all that I set out to do. Over the last year, my dad and mom have worked long hours building their house from the ground floor up. Their dedication, hard work, and perseverance served as an example to me throughout the writing process.

I would also like to Barbara Schmidt-Bailey from the Chicago Board of Trade for providing me with the opportunity to speak at the conference that initially provided me with this book-writing opportunity. At that conference I met Laura Walsh, who was instrumental in putting my passionate views about the commodity markets to paper. I am also grateful for Laura Walsh and Emilie Herman from John Wiley & Sons for their editorial guidance.

As I was writing this book, I had to naturally sacrifice some of my time both at work and outside of work. I want to express my sincere gratitude to Angela and Shane Wisdom for providing me with a work environment that allowed me to write a book in less than six months, and also for their added support along the way. Lisa Hardin was instrumental in reading through my manuscripts and providing accurate suggestions. And Zachary Oxman provided valuable assistance on a wide array of levels.

I would also like to thank Gary Martin, Jerry Needelman, Bill Stephens, and everyone else who provided input along the way. I am also grateful to Peter Schiff of Euro Pacific Capital for providing me with the foundational knowledge about the markets and economy early on in my career.

Outside of work, the countless support, prayers, and words of encouragement from my family, my wife, and friends from Mariners Church kept me going at my moments of weakness. And above all, I am thankful to my Lord Jesus for blessing me with this amazing opportunity.

Commodities for Every Portfolio

Part One

UNDERSTANDING THE COMMODITY MARKETS

Chapter 1

The Long-Term Commodity Boom

Why It's Here and Why It's Going to Last

Teach a parrot the terms "supply and demand" and you've got an economist.

—Thomas Carlye

With the price of oil tripling in value since 2001, gold prices reaching a 26-year high, and a slew of other commodities rising to their highest levels ever, it is not surprising that commodities have become a hot topic of conversation. Even the financial media coverage of commodities has picked up steadily over the last few years. In the past, it was difficult to find stories on the commodity markets. Today you need only to pick up a copy of *The Wall Street Journal* or turn on CNBC to learn about a commodity-related topic. Quite honestly, even the fact that you are reading this book is a testament to the growing interest in the commodity markets.

Yet despite this increased coverage and substantial appreciation, few investors have participated in the gains that these markets have offered over the past several years. The reasons for the lack of participation vary. Some people have readily bought into the fallacy that this is a commodity bubble, while others have simply overlooked this bull market for other investments. At the center of all these reasons is the simple truth that many investors do not understand how the commodity markets work, why commodity prices have escalated over the last several years, and what the advantages are of holding commodities in investment portfolios.

This chapter seeks to establish the case for why we are in the midst of a long-term commodity boom and to focus on the main factors that are instrumental to rising commodity prices. In addition, I elaborate on why it is still not too late to participate in what may be the greatest bull market of our generation. Subsequent chapters in Part One focus on the general makeup of the commodity markets, the common myths associated with commodities, and why commodities belong in every portfolio.

It's a Bull Market

Quite simply, we are in a roaring bull market in commodities. Not a bubble. I want to quickly address this point because many shortsighted economists have argued that the appreciation that has occurred in the commodity markets over the last several years has been nothing more than a bubble created by speculation. It seems that whenever there is a sell-off in the commodity markets, I am called upon by the media to answer the question of whether the commodity bubble has finally burst. My answer, of course, is always the same. This is a certifiable bull market that will last for several years. As long as China keeps industrializing, India continues consuming, and the world keeps on growing, the demand for commodities will grow exponentially over the next several years. Once I get wind that these factors have changed, I might consider changing my position. For now, though, none of these demand factors seems to be close to waning.

In the midst of this growing and soaring demand, the finite amount of raw materials around the world is declining, as expected. A major oil deposit, which typically takes thousands of years to form, has not been found in 26 years. Copper and zinc, two significant industrial metals, are in a supply deficit. The price of sugar, which has always been dictated by food demand, is now heading higher as countries around the world are using sugar to create ethanol, a cheaper and more environmentally friendly fuel alternative. Consequently, the continued supply and demand imbalance facing the commodity markets today will not only propel this bull market further but will also translate to potentially the greatest bull market our generation will ever know.

A Look Back at the Market

In order to fully understand the current bull market, it is necessary to take a look back at the last several years in the commodity markets. At the start of this bull market, gold was trading at $250/ounce, sugar was trading at 5 cents/pound, and the debate was raging over whether crude oil prices would drop below $15/barrel. Interestingly enough, even with the pullbacks that have occurred periodically in the commodity markets, the last several years have been highlighted by prolific gains. Precious and industrial metals have tallied significant returns, the price of sugar moved up four times in value, and the price of oil has had a steady climb to nominal new highs. Indeed, commodities in general have mounted significant gains.

One by one, it seems, commodities have climbed off their bear market lows and appreciated in varying degrees over this first stage of this commodity bull market. At times, the energy sector has led the way; other times, it has been the metals sector. Most recently, the agricultural sector (corn, wheat, soybeans) has led the charge in terms of percentage appreciation.

Reuters CRB Index

Another way to look back at the commodity market is to focus on the Reuters-CRB (Commodity Research Bureau) index. In the same way that the Standard & Poor's (S&P) 500 is a good barometer for tracking the U.S. equity market, the Reuters CRB index is a fairly accurate measure for tracking commodities. There are several more commodity indices out

Table 1.1   Current Reuters–CRB Components

Subgroup	Markets	Subgroup Weight (percent)
Energy	Crude Oil, Heating Oil, Natural Gas	17.6
Grains	Wheat, Corn, Soybeans	17.6
Industrials	Copper, Cotton	11.8
Meats	Live Cattle, Lean Hogs	11.8
Softs	Coffee, Cocoa, Sugar, Orange Juice	23.5
Precious Metals	Gold, Silver, Platinum	17.6

there, but I believe that the Reuters–CRB captures the essence of the first stage of this bull market. The index is made up of 17 commodities that are equally weighted, as shown in Table 1.1.

Several commodities are not represented in the index, but it presents the various types of commodities. For instance, zinc and aluminum are not included in the mix, but copper and platinum are similar in that they are also industrial metals. In any case, since the end of the secular bear market in commodities, the Reuters–CRB index has consistently headed higher. In fact, if a chart could tell a thousand words, Figure 1.1 would aptly describe the commodity markets of the last five years.

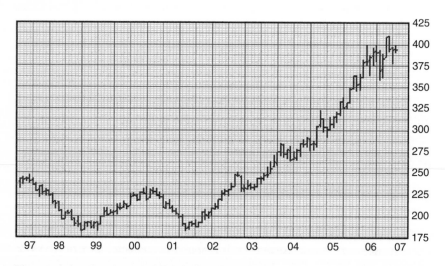

Figure 1.1   Continuous CRB Index (Monthly)
Source: Barchart.com

You can see several things from this chart. If you follow technical analysis, you will likely notice a double bottom formation in 1999 and 2001. From a technical perspective, a double bottom formation is often a clear indicator of a strong uptrend. And sure enough, the Reuters–CRB index has moved up higher since its lows in 2001. The other detail that you should notice is that throughout this move up, there have been several times where the index has had notable declines. In fact, some of these declines have been pretty substantial (greater than 10 percent). What you will notice, however, is that the declines were followed by market rallies that eventually propelled the index to new highs. In some cases, a quick correction was met by a quick recovery; in other cases, the recovery took several months. Nonetheless, this is the nature of any bull market. Pullbacks and consolidations along the way are healthy for the overall direction of the market. As long as the fundamentals are still intact, these pullbacks simply represent a buying opportunity. Take, for example, the gold bull market of the 1970s.

A Golden Example

During the first stage of the 1970s gold bull market, the price of gold moved up from $40/ounce to $199/ounce. The move up, however, did not happen overnight. It took about a couple of years for the price of gold to finally close at just below the $200/ounce level. In 1975 the price of gold then sold off sharply, falling to just below $110/ounce. While this decline was substantial, especially in the moment, it ultimately just represented a correction in a substantial multiyear bull market.

In the 1970s, generally two types of investors participated in the gold market. The first investors purchased gold solely for speculative reasons. In other words, they had seen the price of gold appreciate from $40/ounce and simply wanted to participate in upcoming profits. Beyond this, there was no basis for their purchase. The second investors, however, purchased gold because they understood the fundamentals that were driving prices higher. For instance, these investors understood that the inflationary pressures would only intensify and that demand for the metal would continue to increase. As a result, they were confident that their long-term investment was supported by fundamental factors.

When gold prices corrected from their high, the first investors panicked and sold their positions. In fact, I am sure that many investors happened to get in right at or near the $199 high; this seems to be typical for investors who chase returns. The second investors, however, had a firm grasp on the fundamental factors that were driving the price of gold. Thus, they held on to their positions. In the end, they were able to profit handsomely from a metal that eventually reached $850/ounce in January 1980.

I bring up this example so that you can have an understanding of the dynamics of this commodity bull market. We are in the midst of a long-term bull market that will likely last for another 10 years, but there will also be moments where the commodity markets will experience some pretty significant sell-offs. Does this mean that you should panic? No. Does this mean that the bull market is over? No. As long as the fundamentals are still intact, you can expect commodities to continue their bull run. And it is precisely for this reason that you must understand the fundamentals that are driving this commodity bull market.

A Refresher Course in High School Economics

Believe it or not, it is not too difficult to understand the fundamentals that are driving this bull market. You need only to dust off your old high school economics book and reread the portion about supply and demand. In fact, I will even save you the time. Take a look at Figure 1.2. If the demand of a commodity increases while the supply stays the same or decreases, you can likely expect the price of the commodity to rise. Conversely, if the demand for the commodity decreases and there is more than enough supply to meet demand, the price will likely decrease.

This simple economics equation can be applied to most investments. Take, for example, investing in a signed, limited edition Barry Bonds baseball card. Imagine purchasing this card earlier in Bonds's career. While Bonds was a good player, the demand for the card was not as great as after he broke the record for most home runs in a season. After that feat, the demand for his card increased substantially. More people had an interest in owning Barry Bonds paraphernalia. Consequently, the

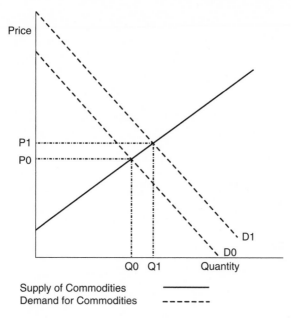

Figure 1.2 Commodity Supply versus Commodity Demand

demand curve moved to the right and the price for the card increased in value.

In the same manner, the main force behind the bull market in commodities has been a growing supply and demand imbalance. In the last several years, the demand for commodities has increased drastically. Simply put, more and more sources of demand have sprouted up that were not around several years ago. This is similar to more people having an interest in owning Barry Bonds paraphernalia. In a normal market environment, the demand in itself would serve as a sufficient catalyst for higher commodity prices. But there is more to this story. At the same time that demand has increased, the supply situation for many commodities has worsened. Can you imagine what would happen to the Barry Bonds baseball card if some of the top-rated cards were burned in a fire? The price of the remaining cards would likely head even higher.

Indeed, this is the situation today in the commodity markets. The price of oil, natural gas, copper, and other commodities has increased because of both rising demand and slowing supply. With that said, I will now address some of these fundamental factors more closely. I start off by looking at the demand side of the equation and then focus on the supply situation.

Accelerating Demand

Many different sources are responsible for this accelerating commodity demand. On one end of the spectrum is the demand from multiple countries that need energy and industrial commodities. On the other end is the growing demand for food, goods, and services by the global consumer. Last is the fact that the world's population is growing at a rapid rate. In a sense, it is almost as if a perfect storm is brewing for commodity demand.

When it comes to evaluating these sources more closely, I encourage you to view things from a big-picture scenario. In other words, consider what these factors will mean for commodity demand five to ten years down the line. Many of the demand sources that have been instrumental during the first stage of this bull market will only accelerate in the years to come.

Growth of Developing Economies

Many of the world's developing economies are responsible for the first part of the increased demand for commodities. Brazil, Russia, India, and China (BRIC nations) have garnered most of the media attention when it comes to their growing commodity demand, but several other countries, mostly in Asia and Latin America, also fall in the developing economies category and have undergone tremendous growth during the first stage of this commodity bull market.

Before looking at the strength of this commodity demand, I want to briefly put into perspective the substantial economic growth that has occurred in many of these developing economies. One way of measuring economic growth is by focusing on the gross domestic product (GDP), which is the total value of goods and services produced by a country. GDP growth will provide you with insight into the economic activity of a given country. In the United States, yearly GDP growth has been around 3 percent. In contrast, the GDP growth for many of these developing economies has been substantially greater (sometimes double or triple the growth rate of developed nations).

As you can imagine, most developing economies have been growing at a substantial rate. In fact, it is no coincidence that the growth of developing economies has coincided with the recent bull market in commodities. This type of economic growth is directly tied in to the fact that these countries are in the process of industrializing their economies. By nature, industrialization begets increased commodity consumption.

Process of Industrialization. At this point, it is important to clarify what usually takes place during industrialization. When most people think about industrialization, they consider it simply as a part of history. In the United States, for instance, industrialization spanned for several decades from the late 1800s to the early 1900s. During that time, the United States (and other western economies) transitioned to manufacturing economies. Beyond that, industrialization is somewhat difficult to grasp because most of us already live in an industrialized nation.

Nonetheless, the process of industrialization is the same regardless of the period during which it happens. During industrialization, agrarian economies transform into industrial or manufacturing-based economies. Factories are built, industries sprout up, cities expand, and the general economic infrastructure is revolutionized. As you can imagine, the transition from farmland to city does not happen overnight. This process typically takes decades to complete. Furthermore, great amounts of raw materials and manpower are needed to build the necessary infrastructure.

Take, for example, the construction of a factory. Besides the energy (oil, natural gas, coal, etc.) that is needed to accomplish this task, basic construction materials are also needed. While I have not been involved in the construction of a large factory, I have had the opportunity to help build a house. I know firsthand the sheer amount of materials that are needed to do so. Cement is needed to create the foundation. Steel, aluminum, and lumber are needed for framing and structure. Copper is needed for plumbing and electrical. You get the picture. Similarly, those same commodities are required to construct factories and buildings in developing economies.

Thailand, India .... In Thailand, for example, the country has transitioned from an economy that relied heavily on exports of agricultural products to an economy that is expanding its manufacturing industries. Both Toyota and Nissan have invested billions of dollars in several projects across the country. Various other industries have also emerged over the last several years. It should be no surprise that steel consumption is growing at a rate of 10 percent in Thailand. Nor should it be much of a surprise that energy demand is expected to double in the next 10 years.

Industrial growth has also been explosive in India. Manufacturing cities, created by the Indian government with the explicit purpose of luring foreign companies, have sprouted up all over the country. Mahindra World City, for instance, is a 1,400 acre special economic zone that has attracted a diverse group of manufacturers. From BMW to Infosys Technologies to Kryoland Cosmetics, these foreign corporations are spending billions of dollars to build factories. Once again, the direct effect of these manufacturing cities and industrial expansions points to the demand for commodities. In India, copper consumption is growing at an 8 percent annual rate.

While the demand for commodities from Thailand, India, and other developing economies has been stellar over the last several years, the trend is by no means over. As long as these countries don't stop midway through their industrialization, I expect commodity demand to continue.

China Factor

Even though China falls into the developing economies category, the country clearly deserves a section all by itself. In a recent television interview, I was asked whether I thought that China was getting too much credit for the rise in commodity prices over the last several years. My response was that China was not getting enough credit. While other emerging nations have increased their demand for commodities over the last several years, none even come close to comparing to China.

In 2004 an article appeared in *The Economist* about China titled "The Hungry Dragon." Beneath the title was a picture of an overweight dragon eating buckets of iron, copper, aluminum, cement, and oil. While the picture was meant to be humorous, it did portray reality. Over the past 15 years, China's demand for base metals (copper, aluminum, zinc, nickel, steel, and iron ore) has tripled. In 1993, China consumed about 7 to 10 percent of the world's base metals. Today it consumes greater than 25 percent.

For most commodities, China is at the top or near the top of yearly consumption. In 2004 China consumed 33 percent of the world's cotton. In 2005 it surpassed Japan as the second largest consumer of oil. In 2006 it was responsible for greater than 50 percent of world's cement demand. Imagine the sheer magnitude of one country consuming more than 50 percent of the world's cement. Not only does this number epitomize the voraciousness of China's commodity appetite, but it also paints a picture of the extent and enormity of China's industrialization.

Indeed, China's industrialization is the linchpin behind its commodity demand. Over the past 20 years, China has transitioned from a heavily agrarian economy into a manufacturing powerhouse. Companies from all over the world have moved either part or all of their manufacturing plants to China. In Shanghai, for example, over 300 of the world's Fortune 500 companies have already set up shop. This number is only going to grow as foreign companies continue taking advantage of China's cheap labor force and growing infrastructure.

With this continued growth in the manufacturing sector, it is no surprise that China's economy is booming. As I pointed out earlier, China's GDP has averaged a yearly growth of 9 percent. Not only has this growth translated into an even greater demand for commodities, but it has also resulted in China's central bank reserves reaching over $1 trillion and growing at a record pace. (See Table 1.2.)

What is most amazing about this economic growth is that it has happened in such a relatively short period of time. To be sure, the speed of China's growth has left the country scrambling for commodities. In the past, China was a net exporter of commodities. In other words, the amount of commodities that China produced was much greater than what it consumed. As a result, China would export these commodities to other countries. Because of the constantly growing commodity demand, China has now become a net importer of commodities. One clear example of this is China's oil production and consumption, shown in Figure 1.3.

Since the early 1990s, China's consumption has been much greater than what it has produced. Undoubtedly, this statistic falls in line with

Table 1.2   China's Central Bank Reserves

Year	US$ (billion)
2001	212.2
2002	286.4
2003	403.3
2004	609.9
2005	818.9
2006	941.1
2007	1000+

SOURCE: State Administration of Foreign Exchange, People's Republic of China

the country's rapid industrialization. Whereas China's production of oil was enough to meet its consumption needs before industrialization, it now has to rely on importing additional oil. And before you think this growth in China is over, think again. According to the United Nations Development Programme, over 300 million Chinese farmers are going to move into the cities within 20 years. This in itself translates to more cheap labor for manufacturing companies, expansion of cities, and the continued growth of the Chinese economy.

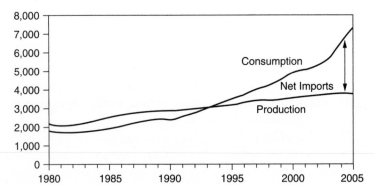

Figure 1.3   China's Oil Production and Consumption, 1980 to 2005 (1,000 barrels/day)
SOURCE: Energy Information Administration

Growth of the Consumer

As you can imagine, the industrialization of emerging economies makes up a significant portion of the increased commodity demand over the last several years. But a question that I am often asked is: what happens once China and other emerging economies complete their industrialization? Does the completion of industrialization signal an end to the commodity bull market? I don't believe it does.

One of the transitions that will occur in the midst of this commodity boom is a shift in the primary demand for commodities. The first stage of this commodity boom is undoubtedly driven by the massive demand for raw materials, such as copper, aluminum, and oil, which are essential in the development of the economic infrastructure. This is why we have seen industrial commodities lead the way in terms of appreciation. The second stage, however, is centered on the growing wealth and spending habits of consumers who reside in most of these developing economies.

This change, of course, is quite logical. One by-product of industrialization is the creation of a wealthier and more educated working class. Therefore, greater than one-third of the world's population (the population in the world's economies) will now have more money to spend: on food, on entertainment, on goods and services that consume commodities. To illustrate this point, imagine this scenario:

In China, a major U.S. company decides to open a manufacturing plant on the outskirts of a city. In order for their plant to run at maximum capacity, they will need to find 2,000 workers. Soon the word is out that the company is paying 20 percent more than what the local farm worker earns. The jobs are immediately filled, and 2,000 people are now making more money. Since most of these workers have no debt, they now have additional income to spend.

With the additional discretionary income comes a change in lifestyle. Some of the workers might eat out more often; others might purchase more expensive food products, such as meat; still others might actually go out and purchase the washer and dryer that they have always wanted. Regardless of their expenditure, the end result is the same. Average Chinese consumers are well on the way to westernizing their lifestyles.

This type of wealth creation will occur not only in China, but in most of the other developing economies. Citizens who typically spend money only on necessary expenditures will begin to indulge in the consumption of goods and services that are standard in most western economies. In fact, if you look at other historical examples of industrialization that occurred in the United States and European countries, a similar type of change took place.

In addition to the spending by these factory workers, there will also be a trickle-down effect as these workers now have more money to spend in the local economy. When they go out to eat, the local restaurant owners benefit. When they buy new clothes or electronic gadgets, local merchants will earn more. In short, the new wealth and spending habits of the factory workers will translate into additional wealth for the business economy. In turn, this will eventually lead to further spending, further growth, and a continued demand for commodities.

As a matter of fact, you can already see this cycle begin to play out in China. The increase in both discretionary income and spending was affirmed in a 2005 survey taken by the National Bureau of Statistics of China. According to the survey, per capita disposable income grew by 11.6 percent year over year. In other words, the average Chinese urban household had additional 11.6 percent more money to spend. Not surprisingly, per capita consumption also increased by 9.8 percent during that time period. Specifically, food expenditures increased by 6.2 percent; clothing expenditures increased by 12 percent; appliances and services expenditures rose by 10.4 percent, transportation and communication expenditures rose by 15.2 percent, and education and entertainment expenditures grew by 11.7 percent.

Indeed, the rise in consumer spending throughout the developing economies is bullish for most commodities. Hard commodities will benefit as the demand for electronics, appliances, and transportation increases. Imagine if the Chinese start trading in their bicycles for automobiles. Not only will there be a greater demand for fuel, but there will also be increased demands for aluminum, copper, platinum, palladium, zinc, and other raw materials that are necessary to build cars. The same can be said for any products that require commodities.

Besides the consumer demand for commodity-based products, there will also be rising demand for agricultural commodities as food expenditures grow. As mentioned, in China, food expenditures increased by 6.2 percent. This increase symbolizes a couple of different things. Not only are Chinese citizens eating more food, but they are spending more money on more expensive food. In other words, instead of relying on diets that are made up of primarily rice, potatoes, and some vegetables, they are now eating more meat and higher-priced agricultural products.

Increased consumption of grain-fed meat and other commodities equates to an increase demand for those commodities. Thus, it should not come as a surprise that over the next several years, many of these developing countries will likely transition from being self-reliant on agricultural commodities to importing commodities from other nations. China has already started this process. In the past several years, it has transitioned from being a net exporter of some agricultural commodities to being a net importer. If you connect the dots, you will easily come to the conclusion that China is now vying for the same bushel of corn that is coming out of the Midwest. As a result, prices will naturally increase.

Global Population Growth

The increase in the global population also has contributed to the demand for commodities over the last several years. Since the mid-1970s, the world's population has increased from 4 billion people to 6.5 billion people (see Figure 1.4). While some people might argue that this trend has been occurring for the last several hundred years, population growth has clearly accelerated over the last century. In fact, the world's population has tripled over the last 75 years. As a result of this exponential population growth, there will be a lot more people competing for the same raw materials.

This demand for commodities will likely occur on multiple levels. Not only will there be more mouths to feed (leading to increased demand for food commodities), but there will be more individuals in need of housing, transportation, basic goods, and services that require energy. Indeed, even when every nation is fully industrialized, global population growth will continue to affect the demand side of the equation.

Another thing that is worth mentioning about the global population is that even as industrialization and wealth creation is occurring in many

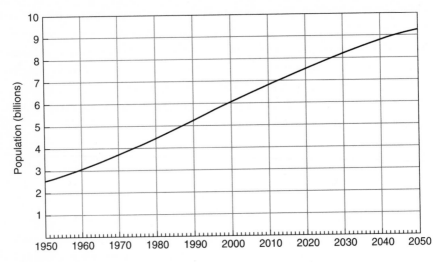

Figure 1.4 Global Population Growth

developing economies, the populations in the developed economies of North America, Europe, and elsewhere are continuing their voracious consumption of commodities. The United States, for example, is still the number-one consumer of oil and many other commodities. Although I will not go into detail about this, suffice it to say that the continued commodity consumption of developed economies is significant and relevant to the demand side of this commodity boom.

Dwindling Supply

Whether it is the industrialization of emerging economies, the massive demand coming out of China, the continual growth of the world's population, or simply the fact that more than one-third of the world is getting richer by the day, the demand for commodities is magnified by the fact that supply is steadily dwindling. In fact, not only is the supply of most commodities dwindling, but we are actually in a supply deficit for some of the world's most needed commodities, such as copper, zinc, nickel, and sugar. A supply deficit occurs when there is more consumption than production of a commodity on yearly basis. When this happens, countries typically tap into their aboveground stockpiles or reserves. However, this is only a temporary fix, not a cure for the problem.

To be sure, the supply situation of most commodities is more dire than just tapping into reserves for a year or two. The dwindling supply is a direct result of the trends that have occurred prior to this bull market, the finite nature of most commodities, and future trends that will occur as a result of industrialization and growth.

Bear Market Blues

One of the key reasons behind the dwindling supply and the subsequent supply deficits in commodities is that we have recently emerged from a multiyear bear market in commodities. From the early 1980s to 2001, commodity prices were at multiyear lows. Oil was trading between $10 and $20 a barrel. Sugar was trading at 5 cents. Gold declined nearly $600/ounce from its 1980 highs. Commodity prices across the board had declined from their previous bull market highs.

While lower prices were a positive thing for consumers, they had a negative impact on producers. With oil trading at $10/barrel, it was not in the best interests for an oil company to spend millions of dollars on oil exploration. With gold prices trading at $300/ounce, it was also not in the best interests for companies to mine for gold. Similarly, other commodity producing companies slowed their investment in future supplies.

The reason for this lack of investment is twofold. First, it is not cost-effective for oil and mining companies to spend money finding new deposits, extracting the deposits, and finally bringing them to the market. Second, many of these companies had experienced falling commodity prices for the better part of two decades. As a result, it was difficult to convince investors (and the companies themselves) that initiating new projects was economically prudent.

Thus, many companies that produced commodities failed to spend the necessary capital looking for future deposits. Of course, the bear market actions of these commodity companies eventually contributed to the shortfall in today's commodity supply. For example, most of the oil fields and mines in production today are a result of exploration that took place several decades ago.

Today, with commodity prices rising to new heights, many commodity-producing companies are upping up their exploration efforts. Oil companies are scrambling to find new oil reserves; mining companies are spending capital exploring for the next mineral find; and in Brazil, acres and acres of sugar are being planted to meet the soaring demand for ethanol. Because of this increased activity and the amount of money being spent on exploration, some pundits will argue that it is only a matter of time before adequate supply will reach the market. When a new oil field is discovered or a new copper mine is in production, supply will meet demand and commodity prices will stabilize or even come down.

This logic, however, fails to take into account several key factors. The first is that it typically takes years for these newfound commodities to be available for use. Consider the oil and gas exploration process. Companies have to first explore and try to find new oil deposits. Then they have to build the necessary infrastructure to extract the oil or gas. Last, they have to refine it and bring it to the market. From start to completion, this whole process can take several years.

The same is true about copper, gold, silver, zinc, and any other metal. Often it can take longer than five years before a mine is in production. Even agricultural commodities can take a while to produce. First, there has to be readily available agricultural land. Second, some commodities take years to produce a crop. For example, it can take three to five years of growth for a coffee tree to yield its first crop. It typically takes a sugarcane plant at least two years to mature. So the next time you are waiting in line for a cup of coffee, think about how long it took for the coffee and sugar to reach you.

The key point to take away from this section is that we have been experiencing rising commodity prices because many commodity producers were singing the bear market blues for too long. In hindsight, this dwindling supply situation could been seen from a mile away. But at the time, no one was looking.

Finite Commodities

Interestingly enough, even if commodity producers did spend money exploring for new deposits and reserves, there would still be no guarantee that there would be enough supply to meet the soaring demand. Why? The answer has to do with the fact that most hard commodities are finite in nature.

By definition, something that is finite does not go on forever. Thus, expecting that we will always be able to find natural gas, silver, coal, or other natural resources to meet the accelerating demand is hopelessly optimistic. Moreover, as much as I would like to do so, I cannot go out and fabricate gold at the local factory. Nor can I create oil at the local laboratory. In short, copper, zinc, iron, lead, platinum, oil, and gas are just some of the commodities that cannot be replenished. As a result, we would expect that these natural resources would deplete over a period of time. And, in fact, this is the case.

For instance, the actual production of oil in the West has declined over the last several decades. There has also not been a major oil find since the Prudhoe Bay oil field was discovered in Alaska in 1968. Why do you think oil is both economically and politically important? Besides oil, other finite commodities have experienced slowing production. The mine supply for gold, for instance, has declined over the last several years.

What puts the finite supply of hard commodities further into perspective is that we really have been consuming most of these commodities only for the last couple hundred years. And some have already reached their production peak.

Lack of Cropland

While soft commodities are not finite, they too have their limitations. One obvious limitation is that you just cannot plant crops anywhere. In China, for instance, only 30 percent of the land is even suitable for farmland. And even if the farmland is available, the terrain or climate might not be appropriate for certain crops. As an example, sugarcane needs a humid, tropical climate in which to grow. Thus, as much as some countries would like to plant sugarcane, they are restricted by their locale. Not surprisingly, as ethanol demand has increased over the last several years, countries have had to rely on Brazil, Thailand, Australia, and other sugar-exporting countries.

The other growing limitation is actually a by-product of industrialization. One of the negatives of industrialization is the fact that expanding cities and towns often replace farmland. In the past decade, over 40 million Chinese farmers have lost their land due to industrialization. In some cases, some of the land was illegally seized and immediately transformed into an industrial or residential area. And as mentioned, 300 million Chinese farmers are expected to leave their farms within the next 20 years. The net result of this transformation is less farmland, fewer farmers, and a smaller supply of agricultural commodities.

Commodity Bubble Argument Dismissed

Despite the fact that the case for investing in commodities is so overwhelming, many Wall Street pundits still argue that we are actually in the midst of a commodity bubble. Some people have even compared the recent move in commodities to the tech bubble of 2000. In truth, this comparison is neither accurate nor realistic. There are some clear differences between the price appreciation of commodities and the tech and dot-com bubble of 2000.

Imagine this dot-com bubble scenario. Say, for instance, that I owned a company. The bulk of my company was an idea, a business plan, and a Web site. My initial investors were willing to put up money and take the risk that the company would eventually be profitable. After a couple of years, the company was still not profitable. However, we had expanded our brand name, took on additional financing, and eventually decided to go public. After the initial public offering (IPO) was filed, the stock started trading at $50 a share. On the first day of trading, the stock moved up to $60 a share. All of a sudden, investors saw that this new "hot" IPO was up 16 percent. Pretty soon investors started piling into this new hot IPO. Eventually the price traded over $100 a share, my company was worth hundreds of millions of dollars, and I was the darling of Wall Street.

Of course, there was no reason or rationale for hundreds of companies to trade at $100 a share. In fact, there was no reason for these companies even to be publicly traded. Nonetheless, the investor euphoria pushed the price of these companies higher. Average people invested in the markets with an unprecedented zeal, some college students invested their tuition money, and a bubble was created. In the end, the bubble burst. Companies went under, paper millionaires were no longer millionaires, and the price of remaining stocks retreated to more realistic levels.

Those who contend that we are in a bubble claim that the same euphoria exists today regarding the commodity market. They claim that it is irrational and illogical that oil is trading at $70 a barrel or that the price of gold is at a 26-year high. Of course, we know that this is not the case. Unlike the dot-com companies that were based purely on hype, commodity prices are a result of a growing supply and demand imbalance. This imbalance is the driving force behind higher prices.

Others have argued that the same speculation and euphoria that drove prices higher during the dot-com bubble are driving commodity prices higher today. Again, there is no truth to this statement. As I stated earlier, most investors are cautious and have not participated in commodity markets over the past five years. This is clearly different from the dot-com bubble when CNBC had record ratings and everyone was sure that the NASDAQ was heading higher. If anything, commodity prices have climbed in the face of pessimism. In the last several years, I have had the opportunity to attend and speak at various investment conferences. I can tell you firsthand that most people have failed to participate in the commodity markets.

Nevertheless, I must also mention that there are times during this bull market when mini-bubbles might form. That is, the price of a commodity might be getting ahead of itself due to excess speculation. Inevitably, the price will correct, speculators will exit, and the commodity will continue with its healthier uptrend. By no means, however, should these corrections be confused with a greater bubble.

Are Commodities Still Cheap?

All of the fundamental factors that I have mentioned can be expanded upon several times over. My purpose in bringing up some of the examples is to lay the foundation for why we have seen commodity prices rise over the last several years and why they will continue to rise in the near future. What makes these markets even more attractive is that commodity prices are still tremendously cheap.

How can this be? How can record oil prices be classified as cheap? Well, the first thing to realize is that comparing the price of a commodity today with the price of a commodity 30 years ago just does not make sense. When the price of oil reached $55 per barrel in October 2004, many proclaimed that oil was at an all-time high. In truth, however, $55-per-barrel oil was only at a *nominal* high. On an inflation-adjusted basis, the price of oil was still below its all-time high.

Confused? Think about it from this perspective. What could $55 buy you in 1980? A whole lot more than it can buy now. Back then, the prices of goods were substantially cheaper than they are today. Thus, in order to find out what the price of a good in 1980 would cost in today's dollars, you have to adjust the price for inflation. To compare with $55/barrel oil in 1980, the inflation-adjusted equivalent price is closer to $100 today.

The same can be said for the commodity market as a whole. Take a look at Figure 1.5, which shows the inflation-adjusted Reuters-CRB Index. As you can see, commodity prices, in real terms, are still cheap.

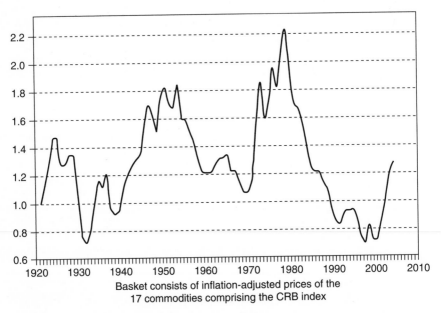

Basket consists of inflation-adjusted prices of the
17 commodities comprising the CRB index

Figure 1.5   Reuters–CRB Index in Real Terms
SOURCE: Di Tomasso Group

We have a way to go before commodities reach their all-time highs. And even if they do reach their real all-time highs, there is a good chance that the prices will likely go even higher.

You can also see this by looking at the chart. Every new commodity bull market has resulted in new real all-time highs. For example, the commodity bull market that started in the early 1930s was eventually surpassed by the bull market of the 1970s. In the same manner, I expect the bull market of today to surpass the bull market of the 1970s.

Conclusion

It is human nature to assume that if you are late to the party, you shouldn't go at all. I have had numerous conversations with individuals who have claimed that they agree with my analysis but they feel that participating in the commodity markets at this juncture is a tad too late. In actuality, it is not too late to participate in this secular bull market in commodities. As impressive as the first stage of this bull market has been, it is only the beginning.

Keep in mind that over the next several years, we will see persistent demand for commodities coming from China, India, and other developing economies. These countries are far from being developed, and the living standards of their citizens are far from those of citizens of developed nations. As these countries play catch-up, there will be continued opportunities to participate in the commodity market.

Chapter 2

From the Farmer to You

How the Futures Markets Work

Reason is the main resource of man in his struggle for survival.

—Ludwig Von Mises

While the commodity futures markets might be new and exotic to most investors, they are by no means new to the financial world. Commodity futures have been around for hundreds of years, providing price stability for goods, a central exchange for trade, and investment opportunities for both hedgers and speculators. Understanding the history and characteristics of the commodity futures market is important if you are looking to fully grasp the dynamics of this bull market. This chapter focuses on the history, makeup, and opportunities that exist in the futures market.

A Brief History of the Commodity Futures Market

Most investors will be surprised to learn that the first recognized commodity futures contract actually began over 300 years ago, near Osaka,

Japan. The Dojima Rice Exchange was established in 1697 with the purpose of stabilizing the price of rice, since the country was constantly at war. Not knowing what the price of rice would be several months down the line, merchants and farmers established standardized contracts between each other, known as rice coupons. Each coupon represented a specific quality and quantity of rice that could be redeemed at a local warehouse for a certain price. Farmers were now able to know how much they would get for their crop, and merchants would be able to count on paying a certain amount for the rice, no matter what happened in a couple of months. These coupons ultimately served to stabilize prices.

It took about another 150 years before this concept caught on in the United States. In 1848 the Chicago Board of Trade (CBOT) was established by 82 businessmen who wanted to have a central gathering place for farmers and dealers. Prior to the founding of the exchange, farmers would bring their crop to Chicago in order find buyers. Since there was no formal and centralized process, farmers would have to travel across the city in search of buyers. Many times farmers were forced to sell their crop at a much lower price, because they did not know that merchants down the road would offer more for the crop.

The CBOT provided a place where all interested buyers could interact with the farmers. Initially, cash, or spot, transactions were most common. Farmers would sell a crop of wheat, corn, or other agricultural commodity on the spot to the highest bidder. Not only did farmers not have to travel around the city looking for buyers, but they were assured that they would get the best possible price. One downside to this transaction, however, was that the facilities that were used to store the grains were above capacity during the harvest months and empty at other times. Because of this drastic fluctuation in supply, spot prices rose and fell in a volatile manner.

As a means to remedy this problem, a number of traders decided to create the "to-arrive" contract. This allowed farmers to receive a pre-established price for their crop, store it at their farmers' locations, and deliver it at a later time. With to-arrive contracts, overcapacity was no longer a problem and volatility in the spot market decreased. Eventually, the to-arrive contract was standardized and became what is now known as the futures contract.

A Closer Look at the Futures Market

Even though the futures market has an extensive history, many investors still do not have a rudimentary understanding of how it works. Still, most people have heard about the futures market in some form. If you watch financial television, you have heard the reporters refer to the futures market and futures contracts. Before the market opens, they often look at what where the Standard & Poor's (S&P) futures are trading at, for a preview of where the market may open. Similarly, when they quote the price of gold, silver, copper, or any other commodity, they use the price associated with the futures market.

Hearing about the futures market is one thing; understanding how it all works is another thing. Here I elaborate on some key aspects of the futures market before I transition to how it all comes together and the opportunity that the futures can offer your portfolio.

Futures Contract

The place to start is with the futures contract. Simply stated, a futures contract is a binding agreement between a buyer and a seller. The seller is responsible for delivering the commodity sometime in the future under a specific set of guidelines. The buyer is responsible for accepting the commodity and paying the pre-established specified amount.

Another way of looking at this is to consider the interaction between a wheat farmer and a baked goods manufacturer. The farmer (seller) wants to lock in a price for the upcoming wheat crop. The baked goods manufacturer (buyer) wants to lock up the price to be paid. From a risk perspective, the farmer wants to get rid of the price risk associated with holding onto the crop of wheat; the buyer wants to make sure not to be at risk of higher wheat prices in the future. As a result, the two establish a binding agreement that assures both parties a specific price at the time of delivery.

In order to ensure maximum price efficiency, each futures contract is standardized. This means that each contract is similar in its quantity, quality, payment terms, delivery month, and delivery location. Since all the contracts that are traded are similar in nature, the variation in price is based strictly on supply and demand factors that are in the market, not the other factors that are specified on the contract. Furthermore, standardization allows for commodities to be traded globally. A buyer in China looking to buy wheat from a farmer in Kansas knows exactly what type of wheat he or she is purchasing.

Once established, futures contracts can also be traded among other investors on a specific futures exchange. This provides investors who are looking to profit from up and down moves in the commodity markets with an investment vehicle that represents the physical commodity.

Futures Exchange

Since the beginnings of the Dojima Rice Exchange, the growth of futures exchanges has increased dramatically. Today there are futures exchanges in North America, South America, Europe, Asia, South Africa, and Australia. The primary function of futures exchanges is to provide an environment for futures contracts and options on those contracts to be traded. In the early days, trades typically took place on the floor of the exchange, where buyers and sellers would trade futures in an open-outcry format (a format defined by shouting and the use of hand signals to communicate trades). Most recently, exchanges have started to transition toward an electronic format where sellers and buyers are electronically matched. In some cases, electronic markets are open day and night. CBOT Gold, for instance, trades 22 hours a day.

Futures exchanges also have specific rules and regulations to which market participants must adhere. The exchanges are responsible for making sure that these rules and regulations are followed. For example, each exchange is responsible for setting the margin requirements for each contract and establishing the daily price limits. This is important, since it serves to control the volatility in the futures market. Additionally, futures exchanges also oversee the day-to-day trading and make sure that business is conducted in an ethical manner.

In turn, futures exchanges also have regulations that they must follow. The Commodity Futures Trading Commission (CFTC) and the National Futures Association (NFA) both monitor the activities that occur at every U.S. futures exchange. In short, futures exchanges are highly regulated exchanges that ensure fair practices.

Besides the Chicago Board of Trade, other recognizable exchanges in the United States include the New York Mercantile Exchange (NYMEX), Chicago Mercantile Exchange (CME), New York Board of Trade (NYBOT), and Kansas City Board of Trade (KCBT).

Participants

There are two participants in the futures markets: hedgers and speculators. Both play an integral role but have a different purpose and function.

Hedgers. Hedgers buy or sell futures contracts in order to lock in the price of a commodity that is supposed to be sold at a later date. In short, hedgers look to sell or buy the physical commodity. Typically, hedgers participate in the market because they are concerned that the price of the commodity might change over the next several months. In order to lock in the current price, they will hedge (or protect) themselves by buying or selling a futures contract on that specific commodity. For instance, if looking at purchasing the commodity in the near future, hedgers will buy the futures contract on that commodity. If the price increases before they are able to take delivery, hedgers will use the gains they made in the futures market as a means to pay the higher price. Alternately, if they are looking at selling the commodity, hedgers will sell the futures contract.

Various strategies are available to hedgers. Unless you are actually looking at buying or selling the physical commodity in the future, you do not really need to know how to hedge. Nonetheless, I still think that is good to have a general understanding of hedging and why hedgers participate in the markets.

Imagine for a second that you are the wheat farmer who is looking at selling your crop to the baked goods manufacturer. For the sake of simplicity, assume that your harvest will yield 100,000 bushels of wheat. When you first plant your crop, wheat is trading at $4 a bushel. In your opinion, $4 a bushel is a good price for your harvest. Unfortunately, your harvest is not yet ready, and you are uncertain whether the price will remain at the current level. Consequently, you decide to hedge your crop by selling short 20 contracts of June $4 wheat.

Since each contract is worth 5,000 bushels, the 20 contracts you sold short represent 100,000 bushels of wheat. Thus, you have effectively hedged your crop. Now, if the price does drop below the $4 level, you are offsetting the loss by making money on your short position.

If the price of wheat moves up to $5 a bushel by the time you are able to sell your harvest, you can still sell your crop at the higher price and use the additional gains to offset your losses in the futures market. The end result, however, will be that you received $4 a bushel for your crop.

As you can see, hedgers participate in the futures market to mitigate risk. In the example, you were willing to pay the amount it cost to purchase the contracts because it would ultimately provide insurance against a much bigger decline. Typically hedgers take this insurance cost into consideration and develop a strategy accordingly.

Speculators. Of course, it takes two to tango, and speculators are the other participants in the futures market. Unlike hedgers, speculators do not participate in the futures market as a way of offsetting risk. In fact, speculators participate in the market in order to profit from the risk that they do take. Speculators use risk capital to profit from movements that occur in the markets.

Ironically, speculators are also looking to profit at hedgers' expense. In the hedging example just described, it is most likely that the speculator buys the 20 futures contracts from you, the farmer. The speculator is actually hoping that price of wheat will rise above $4 a bushel before June delivery. While it might seem paradoxical that speculators are betting against hedgers, their involvement and actions are vital to the futures market. Without speculators, hedgers would not have the ability to hedge.

Several different types of speculators participate in the futures market. Active traders simply look to profit from price discrepancies in the futures markets. Day traders and scalpers both fall into this category. In addition to these more active traders, other traders typically take a position in the futures market because they feel that the fundamentals warrant a much higher or lower price in a certain commodity. For instance, if speculators believe that the price of oil will head higher, they will purchase (go long) oil futures contracts. If speculators believe that the price of oil will decline, they will sell (go short) futures contracts. Regardless of the strategy, speculators provide the futures market with the necessary liquidity.

Most investors who participate in the futures markets are speculators. In essence, in this case you are betting that the price of a commodity will move in a specific direction within a period of time. If you are right, you will make money. If you are wrong, you can lose money. It is important to stress that participating in the futures market involves substantial risk and that it is important to use risk capital only.

Two Tools of the Trade: Leverage and Margin

The amount of money you can make or lose is magnified by the fact that leverage is used in every single futures transaction. In the stock market, if investors wanted to control $50,000 worth of stock, they would have to spend the $50,000. In other words, no leverage would be used in this purchase. If investors wanted to buy 100 ounces of gold coins in the cash market, they would have to pay the full $60,000, if gold is trading at $600/ounce, to control that amount of gold.

This is not the case in the futures market, wherein investors need only a small amount of capital to control a much larger position (leverage). This is why the futures market is referred to as a highly leveraged market. If the price of a commodity rises, you will make more money using leverage. Similarly, if the price of a commodity declines in value, you will lose more money using leverage.

The specific amount of capital that an investor needs to deposit in his or her commodity brokerage account is determined by the initial margin requirement. "Margin" is defined as the amount of money that needs to be deposited in order to take control of one futures contract. Note that the definition of margin in the stock market is different from the definition of margin in the futures market. The phrase "buying on margin" refers to borrowing money to purchase stock. As is often the case with borrowing money, an interest rate (margin rate) is part of the deal.

Margin in the futures market, however, has nothing to do with borrowing money. It merely means how much money you have to put down to take control of a futures contract. Think of it as a down payment of sorts, or a good-faith deposit for the total amount of the futures contract. Using the gold example, if investors wanted to control

100 ounces of gold, they would need to deposit approximately $3,000 in their account. The $3,000 would be leveraged to control a position of 100 ounces of gold.

The exact amount required for margin varies for each commodity futures contract, and it can also change from time to time. The NYMEX and other exchanges are responsible for determining the initial margin requirement. Typically, the initial margin is a percentage of the full contract value (around 10 percent is standard). If the price of a commodity increases in value, the dollar amount per contract is now worth more. Consequently, the exchange will look at increasing the initial margin requirement so that it can stay within that 10 percent range. Conversely, if the price of the commodity decreases, the exchange will look at lowering the initial margin requirement.

Whereas the initial margin is the amount that must be deposited to take control of a futures contract, the maintenance margin is a fraction of the initial margin that must still be on deposit. If the account drops below the initial margin requirement, but not the maintenance requirement, the position can still be held without depositing more money. If, on the other hand, the account falls below the maintenance margin, investors get a margin call. With a margin call, investors have two choices: They can either deposit more money or have the position liquidated. If they deposit more money, the amount has to be sufficient to bring the amount on deposit up to the initial margin requirement.

Futures Trading Involves Substantial Risk

If you have ever received or seen investment information on commodity futures, you would most likely have come across variations of this phrase: "Futures trading involves substantial risk." After reading the sections on speculators, leverage, and margin, you should have a better understanding of why this is the case. Whenever you speculate in the futures market, you have to anticipate that the price will go against you. In other words, there is no guarantee that the price will move in the direction that you would have hoped. Of course, you should be aware of this in any investment that you make. However, this is even more important given the fact that movement in futures markets is magnified by the use of leverage.

How It All Comes Together

So how does all of this come together? How can investors properly profit from participating in the futures market? In Chapter 5, I focus more extensively on how you can invest in commodities by participating in futures. For now, I want to summarize how everything comes together.

Let's assume that you are bullish on the price of copper. After reading my first chapter, you are absolutely convinced that the demand for copper from China and other industrializing nations will only increase over the next decade. While there are some copper mining companies that you can participate in, you decide that you want to participate in more of a pure way. Physically buying the copper and storing it is cumbersome and costly, so you decide to purchase futures contracts on copper. Since you are not a copper miner or a manufacturer that uses copper, you are acting as a speculator in the copper market. In essence, you are speculating that the price of copper will move higher from the current price.

Several exchanges trade copper futures. Investors can purchase copper futures on the London Metals Exchange (LME), the Tokyo Commodity Exchange (TOCOM), and several other futures exchanges worldwide. In the United States, copper futures are traded on the New York Commodities Exchange (COMEX), a division of the NYMEX. Since you will never take delivery on you copper, it doesn't really matter from which exchange you purchase the copper futures. Nonetheless, you decide to purchase copper futures on the COMEX since it is regionally based.

In order to calculate the amount of money you need to deposit per contract, how much copper you will control, and further detailed information, you need to look at the contract specifications for copper. These contract specifications follow.

Trading Unit: 1 contract = 25,000 pounds of copper
Initial Margin: $8,100
Maintenance Margin: $6,000
Price Quotation: cents per pound
Trading Months: There are contracts available for every month going as far out as two years.

Minimum Price Fluctuation: The price of the contracts move up in multiples of five one-hundredths of 1 cent (0.05 cents, or $0.0005) per pound. This is the equivalent of $12.50 per contract. If copper prices move up by 1 cent, that translates into a $250 move per contract.

Last Trading Day: The last day that you can trade the contract is on the third of the last business day of the month that is maturing.

Trading Hours: Open outcry (pit) trading: 8:10 A.M. to 1:00 P.M. Eastern Time. After-hours electronic trading: Monday–Friday: 2:00 P.M. to 8:00 A.M. Eastern Time. On Fridays, the trading concludes at 5:15 P.M. Eastern Time. Trading reopens Sunday at 6:00 P.M.

Source: NYMEX as of 9/1/2006.

As you can see, the contract specification for copper provides you with the information that you need to determine how you will trade.

Now, let's make several assumptions for the sake of clarity. This transaction takes place in September 2006, and we are purchasing the December 2006 futures contract. Let's also assume that the price of December copper is trading a $3.50/lb.

For the sake of simplicity, you decide to purchase one contract of copper. The initial margin you need to deposit in your account is $8,100. Once you purchase the contract, you are in agreement with the seller of the contract (a hedger or another speculator who thinks copper prices will decline) that you will take delivery of 25,000/lbs. of copper at the end of December. In other words, you have leveraged the $8,100 to control $87,500 worth of copper. Keep in mind that only a small percentage of futures buyers ever take delivery. You will actually end up selling your position before the last trading day of the maturing month.

Another aspect of the futures market that is different from the stock market is that your account is debited or credited on a daily basis, known as settlement or marked to market. In the stock market, you do not realize losses or gains until you finally liquidate your position. In any case, the reason why your account is debited or credited daily relates to the contractual relationship between the buyer and the seller.

When the buyer and seller enter into an agreement, they both deposit money in their accounts. Now imagine that the price of December copper moves up by 5 cents, to $3.55/lb. This translates into a $1,250 gain (remember: each cent represents a $250 move). At the end of the day, $1,250 is debited from the seller's account and is deposited into your account. Your account is now worth $9,350. The following day, the price of copper finishes the down 2 cents. Your account is debited by $500, which is credited to the seller's account.

Now let's assume that December copper prices have a sharp sell-off and finish the day at $3.45/lb. This represents a decline of 10 cents, or $2,500 per contract. More important, it represents the fact that your account has declined to $5,600, which is below the maintenance margin requirement of $6,100. At this point, you will receive a margin call and have two options. You can either deposit an additional $2,500 to reestablish the initial margin requirement, or you can liquidate your position. When you purchase a futures contract for any commodity, you are only required to deposit the initial margin amount. However, it is better to deposit a greater amount so that you are not forced with frequent margin calls if the market quickly moves against your position. For instance, if you had deposited $10,000 instead of $8,100, the $2,500 decline would not have incurred a margin call.

If we fast forward to the third week of December, the futures contract is going to expire and the seller is ready to deliver 25,000 pounds of copper. As a speculator, you have no intention of ever receiving delivery on any commodity. Again, if you refer back to the contract specifications of copper, you will notice that the last day to trade copper futures contract for the month of maturation (in this case, December) is the third to last business day of the month. You must offset or liquidate your long December copper futures contract sometime at or before this point.

From a longer-term perspective, you can either go farther out than December or continually roll your contracts to the most current month. To "roll" means simultaneously selling the front month and buying a futures contract for a month farther out. So if you still believed that copper prices were going to increase, you would roll your December contract to a farther-out month.

Other Key Terms to Remember

While the copper example aptly describes how investing in the futures market works, the market has some other key characteristics. The following key terms are prevalent with futures.

Basis, Contango, and Backwardation

It makes sense that the price of a commodity in the cash market differs from the price of a commodity in the futures market. Whereas the spot (cash market) price is determined solely by what the commodity will sell for at that time, the futures price also takes into account additional storage costs, potential supply and demand constraints, and other factors that might alter the price from now until the time of the delivery. Similarly, there is a difference in price for a nearer-term futures contract and a farther-out futures contract. This difference in price between delivery months is referred to as the basis.

When the price of the farther-out futures contract is more expensive than the front month, the future is in what is known as contango. For example, if September corn is trading at 2.40/bushel and December corn is trading at 2.52/bushel, the basis is 0.12/bushel, and corn is in contango. This is normal for most agricultural and soft commodities, since most of the difference in price can be attributed to storage costs. Contango is also common when supply and demand factors are as expected, or status quo.

When supply and demand factors are not status quo, backwardation can occur. Backwardation, the opposite of contango, occurs when future prices are lower in the later months than those in the front month. This scenario might occur if there is an immediate and substantial demand for a commodity. Oftentimes weather-related events and short-term supply disruptions can cause backwardation in the futures market.

Backwardation also occurs when buyers are worried about future supplies and are willing to pay a premium for the nearer-term month. In the summer of 2006, coffee was in backwardation as fears over supply sent the price of front months higher. This was a result of the news that Vietnam, one of the largest producers of Robusta coffee beans, would not deliver supply until November and that its crop was the smallest in three years.

While basis, backwardation, and contango are most useful to active traders and hedgers, the terms can also give investors insight into current economic factors in the markets. As you can see, the news of slower supply from Vietnam was immediately reflected in the futures market.

Short Selling

For those of you who are not familiar with selling short, it is basically the opposite of going long. When you are long a position, you are hoping that the price will head higher. When you are short a position, you are hoping that the price of the commodity will head lower. In the futures market, it is just as easy to go short a commodity as it is to go long. For instance, if you believed that the price of copper would actually decline by December, you would sell short one contract of copper at $3.50/lb. If the price eventually declined to $3.00/lb., you would offset your short position by buying back one December copper contract at $3.00/lb. The net result would be a profit of 50 cents/lb., or $12,500.

So what does short selling mean for you? First, it allows you to profit from downward moves in the commodity markets. At times, there will be opportunities where a specific commodity is overvalued. If you believe that the commodity will decline in price, you can sell it short. The other advantage of the ease of short selling is that it allows you to participate in the commodity markets during both bull and bear markets. Looking back at the previous bear market in commodities, investors had many opportunities to short.

Options on Futures

Investors can also participate in the futures markets by purchasing or selling options on futures. This is similar to purchasing or selling options on stocks. Buyers pay sellers of an option a premium for the right to purchase the futures contract at a specified price within a certain period of time. If the option expires worthless, buyers lose the premium they paid for the option. If the option is in the money, buyers receive the futures contract at the specified price.

If you are interested in learning more about options, I urge you to read more about it. In Chapter 12, I discuss some different avenues that you can take to learn more about futures, options on futures, and other tools and strategies that can help you in your investment decisions. For now, let's just say that options on futures are another way that you can participate in the futures market.

How the Commodity Futures Market Benefits *You*

As you can see, the makeup of the futures markets is pretty straight-forward. It is a constant interaction between speculators and hedgers, farmers and baked goods manufacturers, mining companies and metal fabricators, and a wide array of other participants who have an interest in the various commodity markets. The constant interactions between buyers and sellers provide for a central marketplace of trade and make the futures market highly liquid and transparent.

A Highly Liquid, Efficient, and Transparent Marketplace

The liquidity of the futures market makes it easy for investors to enter into and exit out of futures contracts. If you are looking at closing out one of your futures positions, you should not find it difficult to find a buyer (or a seller). The advent of electronic markets and trading has added further liquidity to the marketplace. Investors are now able to participate in the futures market virtually around the clock in a number of exchanges worldwide.

While the liquidity of the markets provides logistical benefits for futures investors, the more important benefit is that of price discovery. In a nutshell, price discovery is the process by which the price of a commodity is accurately displayed in the futures market. This is a result of the liquidity, continual flow of information, and the transparency that occurs in these markets.

If you remember, futures contracts are standardized. Since the quantity, quality, and delivery are all the same, the movement in prices is strictly dependent on the actual or expected changes in the supply and demand factors of a specific commodity. For example, in August 2006, the United States Department of Agriculture issued a report that stated that the corn supply was larger than expected. The expectation that supply would outstrip demand was immediately reflected in the price of corn. As a result, corn prices declined sharply over several days. Similarly, the threat of a Category 4 hurricane off the coast of Florida in 2005 sent orange juice futures prices skyrocketing. The market immediately anticipated destruction of supply, and the price of orange juice futures climbed to multiyear highs.

As you can imagine, when billions of dollars are traded in a highly liquid and transparent marketplace, investors on both sides of the contracts will make calculated decisions on where they feel the price of a commodity should be. Weather-related events, agricultural reports, geopolitical tensions, and long-term demand from China are all factors that are reflected in the futures markets. Not only do these accurately reflected prices provide hedgers with maximum efficiency, but they also provide speculators (you) with a pure way of following and investing in the commodity markets.

A Pure Way to Follow and Invest in Commodities

Indeed, no other market in the world provides investors with as clear of an outlook on commodities as the futures market. Quite honestly, no other market even comes close. Commodity-related stocks, for example, have other variables that distract from the actual price movement of the commodity. It might be that you have been following the price of a gold company, only to find out that it was hedging its gold output. The cost to hedge ultimately subtracted from the profits of the company. Perhaps you have been looking at an oil company that recently stated that it has less oil than it initially thought it had. Its stock price dropped even as the price of oil continued heading higher. No matter the company, management issues, earnings, accounting, and other factors will only detract from the actual commodity that it is representing. Even if you use the futures market merely as an educational source, it is in your best interest to understand how it works.

More important, the futures market offers investors the opportunity to profit from this bull market in commodities. While the concept of futures was established to create price stability for rice farmers, ultimately futures have provided investors with a way of directly participating in the commodity markets. If you understand the makeup and risk associated with the futures market, participating in it is the most tangible way of experiencing bull market growth.

Conclusion

It is actually quite impressive that the history of futures markets spans several hundred years. From their humble beginnings in Japan to their present-day significance across multiple continents, futures markets have evolved to provide investors from all over the world with the ability to participate and profit from movements in commodity markets.

The history and function of futures markets provides the backdrop for you to understand why we are in the midst of this commodity bull market.

Chapter 3

Debunking Commodity Myths

Why Commodities Belong in Your Portfolio

The great enemy of the truth is very often not the lie—deliberate, contrived and dishonest—but the myth—persistent, persuasive and unrealistic.

—John F. Kennedy

A s is the case with most myths, the source of the misconceptions about commodities can be traced to misinformation and lack of knowledge. After reading the first two chapters of this book, you probably know more about the commodity markets than most investors. Most people, however, still lack a basic understanding of the futures markets. Instead of picking up a book and educating themselves about the world's hottest markets, they rely on misinformation that is passed along from other sources. A friend of a friend might have relayed a horror story about how he lost money investing in gold or oil. A financial advisor might have cautioned against investing in commodities.

Perhaps a CNBC guest proclaimed that commodities were too risky for investors.

In all of these cases, a good number of assumptions were made along the way. Take for example, the seemingly common friend-of-a-friend story. Often the facts behind the story are left out. What trading strategy did the friend implement? Was he overly aggressive? Did he even know what he was doing? Instead, the focus is simply on the fact that he lost money trading commodities. Pretty soon the story is told over and over again, and the myth that you will definitely lose money trading commodities is created.

Over the past several years, I have personally heard the friend-of-a-friend stories and countless other myths about the commodity markets. Truthfully, I am surprised that so many myths surround a market that has been in existence for hundreds of years. In addition, I would think that there would be more clarity surrounding a market that is so vital to the financial makeup of world economies. Unfortunately, this is not the case. The continual reiteration of the commodity myths have kept investors from truly experiencing the benefits of investing in commodities.

The purpose of this chapter is twofold. First, I debunk some of the most common myths that surround the commodity markets today. Then I highlight four of the key reasons why commodities should be a part of every investor's portfolio.

Debunking the Myths

One of the main reasons why I wanted to follow up the chapter that discussed the makeup of the commodity markets with some prevailing myths about commodity futures is because I have learned that even people who understand how commodities work still believe some of the myths. Although many possess an academic understanding of these markets, these myths prevent them from participating.

The myths that I listed before are a few that are pretty common. Some of these might seem unbelievable, but I can assure you that numerous people do believe them.

Myth #1: You Will Lose Your Shirt Trading Commodities

The belief that you will inevitably lose your shirt trading commodities is perhaps the most common myth associated with these markets. If *Family Feud* asked 100 people what came to mind when they thought about commodities, I would not be surprised to see the number-one answer having to do with how commodities are too risky.

This logic, however, is flawed. While it is true that you can lose money trading commodities, you can also lose money investing in stocks, homes, antiques, and even Barry Bonds baseball cards. If I purchased a house at the peak of the real estate market, I would most likely lose money on the investment. Does this mean that I shouldn't invest in real estate again? No. It just means that I purchased it at the wrong time. Next time I should spend more time researching the current market environment for real estate.

In the same way, if you participate in the commodity markets, you have to realize that both risks and rewards are associated with your investments. Furthermore, whether you make or lose money in these markets is strictly dependent on your trading decisions. By and large, the investors who "lose their shirts" trading commodities fail to implement prudent money management or are too aggressive in their trading.

Later on in the book, I present some money management techniques and trading strategies that investors can implement. For now, I want to point out that most of the stories about losing your shirt are generally a result of poor money management and investment decisions.

Moreover, it is important to know that the futures market is a zero-sum game. That is to say, for every person who loses money trading the futures contract, there is a winner. How does this work? Think about it from the perspective of the futures contract. You purchase a futures contract from a seller. If the price declines and you lose money, the person who is short the contract makes money. Conversely, if the prices appreciate, you make money and the person who sold the contract loses money. The point that I am trying to make is that for every circumstance where an individual lost her shirt, there was someone who gained from that investment.

Myth #2: Commodities Are More Volatile than Stocks

The belief that commodities are more volatile than stocks is also an ongoing myth. In simple terms, volatility measures the fluctuation in the price of a stock, futures contract, or other type of investment over a short period of time. For example, if the price of oil does not fluctuate much over a period of time, it exhibits low volatility. However, if the price of oil fluctuates widely (up $3, down $5, up $2, etc.), it exhibits high volatility.

While volatility is a good thing for active traders, most investors prefer not to have a highly volatile portfolio. On a recent airplane flight I happened to sit next to a financial advisor who believed strongly in asset allocation. He proceeded to tell me about his recommended portfolio, which, not surprisingly, did not include an allocation toward commodities. When I asked him why he didn't recommend holding commodities, his response was that his clients would not want the volatility associated with the commodity futures markets.

Ironically, his stock-heavy portfolio would have had greater historical volatility over a lengthy period of time than if he had invested in commodities. In 2004 Gary Gorton of University of Pennsylvania and K. Geert Rouwenhorst of Yale School of Management shattered the myth that commodities were more volatile than stocks, when they published "Facts and Fantasies about Commodities." The Yale study examined the characteristics of the commodity futures market from July 1959 to December 2004.

In one section, Gorton and Rouwenhorst looked at the risk and return of commodity futures versus the risk and return of stocks and bonds. During this 45-year period, they concluded that the risk premium for stocks was slightly higher than that for commodity futures. In other words, your portfolio would have been more volatile invested in stocks than in commodity futures.

Although this fact might startle some investors, it can easily be confirmed by looking back at market dynamics of the past 45 years. There have been times when commodities have exhibited greater volatility than stocks; however, there have also been times where stocks exhibited greater volatility than commodities. The recent tech bubble is a prime example of great volatility in the stock market. Many tech stocks appreciated and depreciated in a volatile manner over a period of a couple of years. During that same time period, the CRB index appreciated much more steadily and gradually. As a result, investors would have been exposed to less volatility if they had invested in commodity futures.

Therefore, concluding that commodities are more volatile than stocks is purely a myth. While there are undoubtedly times when this might be true, a longer perspective shows that this is not truly the case.

Myth #3: Commodities Are Only for the Very Wealthy

For some reason, there is also a prevailing myth that commodities are only for the very rich. Perhaps this has something to do with the increasing focus on hedge funds. Stories abound about how hedge funds typically take large positions in commodity markets. Since most hedge funds cater to institutions and high-net-worth individuals, I would imagine that some investors might assume that they can't participate. And in some cases this is true; investors must have a certain net worth to qualify for a certain investment.

Of course, this is not the case for all commodity funds or commodity investments. Several futures-based funds allow investors to participate at a much lower minimum than what many hedge funds would require. Additionally, if investors wanted to trade commodity futures themselves, they can easily accomplish this by opening a commodity brokerage account and trading single contracts on specific markets. If you remember, it takes under $4,000 to purchase a contract of gold. Some agricultural commodities have even lower margin requirements.

Therefore, commodities are not only for the very wealthy. These days commodity funds or other types of pooled investments provide exposure across a wide range of commodities for only a fraction of the amount you would normally need to invest individually in all of those commodity markets.

Myth #4: Commodities Are Difficult to Understand

There are a number of different reasons why people believe the myth that commodities are too difficult to understand. For some, it's a simple case of knowing what they see. If most of the investment world focuses on stocks and bonds, then they will not bother to learn about the commodity markets. Others might fall back on a horror story they once heard about commodity futures. Still others might falsely assume that just because stocks and futures have different characteristics and definitions, futures are more difficult to comprehend. Whatever the reason, it is clear that many people believe this myth.

Truthfully, I don't understand why people have this viewpoint. Not only are commodities not difficult to understand at all, they are much simpler to follow than stocks. Think about it from this perspective: If you are doing research on a specific stock, you have to look at a number of different factors. What is the stock's price to earnings ratio? Have sales increased year over year? What about the company management? Are they qualified to take the company to the next level? What about the competition? Investors look at all of these factors and more to determine the potential direction of the price of a stock.

In comparison, investors who are following a specific commodity need to focus only on the supply and demand factors that might alter the price. With commodity futures, there are no management issues, no accounting irregularities, no earnings season. You simply have to stay abreast of factors that might alter the supply or demand part of the equation. For example, if you wanted to invest in corn, you might want to look at the current level of supply, the upcoming crop potential, and the level of demand over your specific time horizon.

Equally important is the fact that most people interact with commodities on a daily basis. If you really stop and think about it, most of what average people spend their money on revolves around the consumption of commodities. When you wake up in the morning, you might drink a cup of coffee. On the way to work, you might put gasoline in your car. When you pay your electric bills, buy a car, buy clothes, or even bake a cake, you are spending money on commodity-related expenses. The prices of these items are dependent on the prices of the physical commodities. For instance, when crude oil prices rise because of increased tensions in the Middle East, you can easily see this in gasoline prices. When excessive heat drives up demand for natural gas, you can also see this in your utility bill.

If you really take time to focus on your day-to-day interaction with commodities, I firmly believe that you will gain a greater understanding of this commodity bull market. Next time you are standing in line at Starbucks, think about the price of coffee. Notice how many people religiously order their nonfat vanilla lattes every morning. Now imagine what the demand for coffee from industrializing economies will do to that price.

Myth #5: Investing in Commodities Makes Sense Only If We Are in a Bull Market

Another common myth that I have heard is that commodity investments make sense only when commodity prices are heading higher. If the bull market in commodities continues, then you should invest. If, however, commodity prices start declining, you should exit the commodity markets altogether. Again, this idea is based on a lack of knowledge. If you firmly believe that the price of a specific commodity will decline, you can just as easily sell short the commodity and profit from the decline. If you don't believe me, just ask George Soros. In 1992 this billionaire investor shorted the British pound and was able to pocket a cool $1 billion in a single day. While this experience is extraordinary, I use it to point out that investors can make money in declining commodity markets.

The other factor that is important to consider is that commodities also make sense as a portfolio diversifier. In other words, whether we are in a bull market, bear market, or sideways market, commodities can still benefit your portfolio. I elaborate on this point later in this chapter.

Myth #6: Commodities Are All about Orange Juice and Pork Bellies

"So you are a commodity broker? Can I buy some pork bellies and orange juice?" For whatever reason, I have heard versions of this comment several times over at different social engagements. Many people believe that commodities are all about orange juice futures or pork belly futures. In a way, it reaffirms the myth that commodities are exotic and not for every investor. I mean, why would anyone want to invest in pork bellies?

The truth of the matter is that commodities are *not* all about orange juice and pork bellies. The commodity markets are wide and diverse and provide investment opportunity on a variety of levels. In Chapter 5 I list some of these markets to give you an idea of their diversity. You will see that those who participate in these markets are not only investing in exotic commodities, they are investing in real assets that are vital in the global economy.

Keep in mind that these are just some of the myths. Undoubtedly there are a good many others that I haven't mentioned. The only way to determine whether something is a fact or a myth is to fully educate yourself about the commodity markets. I am quite sure that after reading through the first couple chapters, you have already had an "oh . . . I didn't know that!" moment.

Commodities for Every Portfolio

Earlier in the chapter, I briefly touched on the study conducted by Gorton and Rouwenhorst. It was not only instrumental in debunking several commodity myths, but it also served to define the relationship among the three different asset classes: commodity futures, stocks, and bonds. More important, Gorton and Rouwenhorst were able to show that there were obvious advantages to adding commodity futures to a typical stock and bond portfolio.

The two professors began their study by constructing an equally weighted performance index of 35 commodity futures, which was supposed to represent the commodity futures market. The historical return of the index was then compared against the historical returns of the Standard & Poor's (S&P) 500 total return index and the Ibbotson corporate bond total return index. After comparing the monthly returns of the indexes over a 45-year period, they concluded that stocks and commodity futures ultimately performed the same. During that same time period, corporate bonds underperformed both of the other asset classes.

Initially, reading that commodities and stocks have had similar performances over the last 45 years might be confusing, especially since most recently stocks have clearly outperformed commodities. However, if you look at Figure 3.1, you can see that there have been various times

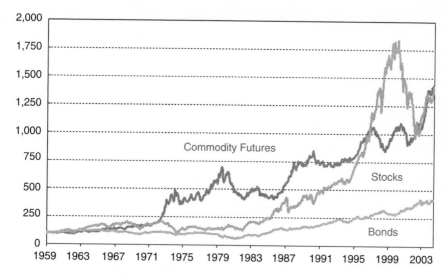

Figure 3.1 Long-Term Performances of Stocks, Bonds, and Commodity Futures

SOURCE: Gary B. Gorton and K. Geert Rouwenhorst, "Facts and Fantasies about Commodity Futures," *Financial Analysts Journal* 62, No. 2 (April 2006): 47–68

when stocks and commodities have alternated in performance. For instance, commodities outperformed stocks during the 1970s, and stocks outperformed commodities during the 1990s.

Over a prolonged period of time, commodity futures were negatively correlated with stocks and bonds. In other words, commodities and stocks typically moved in opposite directions. One way of understanding why this is true is to focus on the effects that commodity prices have on companies.

Typically, when commodity prices decline, it becomes much cheaper for companies to manufacture goods. The cheaper goods are then more readily purchased by the consumer, earnings grow, and stock prices rise. Higher commodity prices, however, have a negative impact on companies. Companies are now paying more for commodities, the consumer is paying more for goods, and stocks suffer as earnings decline.

Gorton and Rouwenhorst also reported that while commodity futures were negatively correlated to stocks, they were positively correlated with inflation. During periods of high inflation, such as the 1970s, commodity prices soared. Conversely, during periods of low inflation, such as the 1990s, commodity prices declined. In comparison, stocks and bonds were negatively correlated with inflation.

Commodities in *Your* Portfolio

While the preceding synopsis might come across as a statistical research report, it also serves to reaffirm several of the main reasons why you should have commodities in your portfolio.

Before I go into how commodity futures can help enhance your portfolio, I must first point out that not all investor portfolios are alike. The actual composition of any portfolio is based on a number of different factors. One of those factors is the risk profile of investors. For instance, if investors are primarily concerned with capital preservation, having a portfolio that is heavily weighted toward commodities might not make the most sense. Similarly, if investors desire above-average returns, a portfolio that is made up mostly of bonds will likely not accomplish this objective. The goal is to construct a portfolio that meets your objectives, limits your overall risks, and maximizes your returns. While all of the reasons that I discuss next are advantageous, one or more might carry a greater significance for your portfolio.

Commodities as a Diversifying Asset Class

Most investors understand the value of diversification. The general premise is that you can lower your overall portfolio risk if you spread your capital among a variety of investments that move in opposite directions. The logic behind this is that some of your investments might do well in a specific market environment, while other investments might appreciate in a different market environment. By diversifying your portfolio among different investments, you typically get a much more balanced and less volatile portfolio.

The key to diversification, however, is finding investments that are negatively correlated to each other. Investments are negatively correlated if they move in opposite directions. Conversely, investments that are positively correlated move in the same direction. Unfortunately, many investors today have mistaken diversification for variety. In other words, just because you have a portfolio of 100 stocks that are spread among various market sectors does not mean that you are truly diversified. Imagine what would happen if we suffered a stock market crash or a prolonged bear market in equities. Your portfolio of stocks would not be as diversified as you would think.

By adding commodity futures to your portfolio, you are adding an asset class that is not correlated with your other stock and bond investments. As a result, if the prolonged bear market scenario transpires, at least a portion of your portfolio is in an asset class that historically has thrived in that market environment. Even if you argue that that scenario will not occur, you are still lowering your risk by spreading out your investments over a negatively correlated asset class.

One of the earlier believers in using commodities as a diversifying asset class was Jack Meyer, the former head of Harvard University's endowment program. In an article that was published in *The Wall Street Journal* in November 1996, he stated: "Holding commodities offers protection against the ups and downs of stocks and bonds." He then went on to say that commodities are "the most diversifying asset class in the portfolio."

Commodities as a Hedge against a Bear Market in Stocks

If you are concerned about a bear market in stocks, it should interest you to know that commodities can serve as a hedge against such a market. Truthfully, there is more than a distinct possibility that we will be in a prolonged equities bear market. If stocks and commodity futures are negatively correlated, and we are in a commodities bull market, then we can assume that we are in the midst of a bear market in stocks. Wait, you say. How can this be? Hasn't the stock market appreciated consistently over the last several years?

Indeed, the stock market has appreciated over the last several years. However, the appreciation, in my opinion, was nothing more than a multiyear rally in a bear market that started in 2001. Consider this argument. After the dot-com and tech bubble burst, one would imagine that investors would cut back on their lavish spending, start saving money, and atone for their financial mistakes. History has shown us that this is what typically occurs after most bubbles. However, this scenario did not take place.

Of course, if you are a homeowner, you probably understand why this is the case. The artificially low interest rates and exotic mortgages provided a catalyst for increased demand, which ultimately pushed home prices much higher than they should have been. In turn, the higher home prices provided investors with an opportunity to refinance their homes, take cash out, and ultimately continue spending money in the economy. Not surprisingly, consumer spending and housing-related industries helped provide a boost to the beleaguered equities market.

Unfortunately, this boost turned out to be only a temporary shock to a fundamentally flawed stock market. As the housing market continues its deceleration, as consumer spending stalls, and as interest rates inevitably rise, the downward trend of the stock market will once again accelerate. And remember, even if we have an economic slowdown in the United States, commodity demand will still be strong from China and other developing nations.

Whether you agree with this analysis or not, it still makes sense to have a portion of your portfolio in futures that will protect you against the downturn in the market. Indeed, hedging your portfolio with an exposure to commodities can bring noncorrelated returns during periods of a declining stock market.

Commodities Can Protect Your Portfolio against Inflation

While inflation is caused by an increase in the money supply (otherwise known as printing money), inflation is generally defined as the rise in the price of goods and services. Another way that people often look at inflation is as too much money chasing too few goods. When this occurs, it takes more of your money to buy the same amount of goods. Some economists disagree on how to properly measure inflation. The government, for instance, typically focuses on the core Consumer Price Index (CPI) to gauge the level of inflation. Others argue that the core CPI is inherently flawed, since it does not take into account food and energy prices. Regardless of your definition, most people can at least agree that the effects of inflation can wreak havoc on both stocks and bonds.

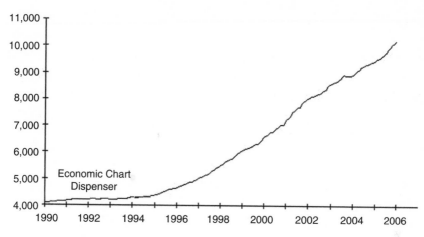

Figure 3.2 M3 Growth (billions of dollars)
SOURCE: www.economagic.com

The massive inflation that occurred in the 1970s is a prime example of this. If you look back to Figure 3.1, you will see that during that decade, stocks and bonds were both in a bear market. Of course, Gorton and Rouwenhorst confirmed that inflation is negatively correlated with stocks and bonds. So what about today? What is the likelihood that we will have inflation that is similar to what we experienced in the 1970s?

I personally think the likelihood is quite high. Consider all the events that have transpired over the last several years: the creation of the U.S. Department of Homeland Security, the wars in Iraq and Afghanistan, Hurricane Katrina. All of these events require a tremendous amount of money. Unfortunately, the only way to pay for it all is to expand the money supply. Figure 3.2 shows the expansion of the money supply, which is measured by M3, over the last several years.

All of these expenditures, including the general creation of more money by the United States and other countries, have created a scenario in which a lot more money is chasing around too few goods. Consequently, commodity prices have become more expensive. It is only a matter of time before the higher commodity prices are eventually passed on to the consumer.

I must say that this pass-through effect of higher commodity prices does not have to happen immediately. In fact, some companies must lock in the price of product several years out. Once I had the opportunity to sit down with an executive of a small appliance manufacturing company. He relayed to me that the rising cost of copper, zinc, and nickel had adversely affected the company's bottom line. When I asked why he didn't just raise his prices, he stated that he had a multiyear contract with a larger wholesaler that locked in the price.

Common sense dictates that most companies are in the business of making money. This small appliance manufacturer and thousands of other companies will eventually charge more for their goods. In the case of the executive, he was considering buying futures contracts to hedge the inflating copper, zinc, and nickel prices.

Investors can also hedge their portfolio by participating in commodity futures. Concern about maintaining the purchasing power of your wealth is probably one of the more important reasons why you would want to have commodity futures in your portfolio.

Commodity Futures for Greater Returns

Some investors could care less about portfolio diversification, lowering their risk, or hedging themselves against inflation. These investors are more concerned with investing their capital in something that makes sense and will likely appreciate over a period of time. Fortunately, commodity futures also provide investors with an opportunity to profit from the greatest bull market our generation will ever know. The upward movement of the commodity markets will be magnified by the leverage component of futures contracts. Remember, though, that while leverage can provide investors with above-average returns, it can also result in above-average losses. It works both ways.

Even if you agree with the bull market in commodities but prefer to invest in commodity stocks, you should know that commodity futures typically appreciate more than their stock counterparts. In their extensive study on the futures markets, Gorton and Rouwenhorst also compared the performance of commodity futures with the same type of commodity stocks. Their conclusion was that over a 41-year period (1962–2003), you would have had greater returns had you invested in commodity futures.

Thus, commodity futures markets provide you with the opportunity to earn above-average returns.

Conclusion

Commodities belong in every portfolio. While the myths surrounding these markets might seem credible initially, they are easily discredited when you understand the facts about the commodity futures markets. Furthermore, the diverse and unique characteristics of the futures markets provide several reasons why investors should allocate a portion of their portfolio to commodity futures. If you are a risk-averse investor who values diversification, commodities might make sense for you. If you are concerned about the current state of the stock market or the ever-growing rate of inflation, commodities can serve as a hedge against the rest of your portfolio. Even if you are only looking at the futures markets as a path to participate in this roaring bull market, commodities can provide you with the ability to have greater returns.

Part Two

PARTICIPATING IN THE COMMODITY MARKETS

Chapter 4

Deciding What Is Right for You

Futures, Stocks, Mutual Funds, and Exchange-Traded Funds

A little knowledge that acts is worth infinitely more than much knowledge that is idle.

—Khalil Gibran

At this point, you should have a great deal more knowledge about the current bull market in commodities, the general makeup of the commodity futures markets, and the distinct advantages that commodity futures can add to your typical stock and bond portfolio. For some of you, all of this information was just a reaffirmation of what you already knew. For others, most of this information was surprisingly eye-opening.

Whatever your reaction to the first part of the book, it should be clear that understanding the commodity markets is only the first step in the investment process. The second step is actually participating in these markets. And the final and most important step is profiting from it all.

Fortunately, there is still ample time to participate and profit from this long-term commodity boom. Developing economies are far from being developed, the consumer-driven demand for commodities is steadily increasing, and supply constraints will only intensify over the next several years. In addition to all of these factors, participating in this commodity boom has never been easier. Besides futures, investors can profit by investing in stocks, mutual funds, exchange-traded funds (ETFs), and even commodity currencies.

This part of the book focuses on the different ways that you can participate in the commodity markets. Specifically, I examine how rising commodity prices positively benefit investment vehicles and how you can use them to profit from this long-term commodity boom. The chapters in this part look at these investment vehicles in greater detail. However, before I delve into these specifics, I think it is important to understand how each individual vehicle relates to the current bull market in commodities. Once you understand this, you can decide which vehicle to use to profit from rising commodity prices.

Commodity Futures Revisited

It should come as no surprise that commodity futures are at the top of my list when it comes to participating in the commodity markets. No other investment vehicle provides investors with as pure and direct a way to participate in this commodity bull market. When you purchase a commodity futures contract, you are directly participating in the commodity marketplace. On any given trading day, you can enter into an agreement with a wheat farmer from Kansas City or a silver producer from Idaho. You can purchase an oil contract alongside a multinational corporation or sell a gold contract to a gold jewelry manufacturer in India. This direct interaction with commodities is quite simply the purest way of participating in this commodity boom.

Futures Focus

There are several other reasons why I focused so extensively on the futures markets in Part One. The first reason has to do with the general lack of understanding about the commodity futures markets. I firmly believe that in order to fully understand the dynamics of this commodity boom, you have to understand how the futures markets work. In other words, knowing the history, function, and purpose of the futures markets will provide you with better insights on why commodity prices move the way they do.

If you stop and think about it, this makes perfect sense. Commodity prices move up or down based on the activity that occurs in a given futures market. At times, this movement might occur because speculators are anticipating higher prices down the line. Other times commodity prices appreciate due to increased demand from consumers. Whatever the reasons, as long as you understand the players involved and what the futures markets represent, you can more easily follow the factors that affect this commodity bull market.

The second reason is a bit similar to the first one. I have had too many interactions with people who automatically tune out anything commodity related because they had a preconceived idea about the futures markets. Thus, I believe it was important to debunk some of the most popular myths before writing about how investors could actually participate in the commodity markets. My hope is that now that you understand that commodities are a viable investment, you can focus more clearly on the different commodity options.

Finally, the commodity futures markets have an effect on most of the other commodity-related investments, and therefore they must be discussed. When you look at commodity stocks, for example, they often move in tandem with their underlying commodity futures contract. On days that oil futures are moving higher, you will find a vast majority of oil-related companies also moving higher. The same can be said about commodity mutual funds and commodity Exchange Traded Funds (ETFs). Even commodity currencies often fluctuate with rising or falling commodity prices. Consequently, understanding the commodity futures market, regardless of whether you invest in it, allows you to have a better grasp of the other commodity-related investments.

Advantages of Futures

Commodity futures do have certain advantages in their own right. In fact, some of these advantages are what distinguish commodity futures from the other investment vehicles. The first advantage, of course, has to do with the fact that you are investing in the actual commodity. As I mentioned, a commodity futures contract represents a specific amount of the physical commodity. For instance, when you purchase a sugar contract—say, NYMEX No. 11 sugar futures—you know exactly that you are purchasing a contract that represents 112,000 pounds of sugar. In contrast, buying a commodity mutual fund or a commodity stock does not directly expose you to the physical commodity. Nor does it expose you solely to that single commodity. The performance of those other investment vehicles depends on a number of factors, such as the skill of the fund manager or the profitability of the company. With commodity futures, performance is strictly dependent on the performance of the real asset.

Another advantage of commodity futures is that they provide you with the opportunity to invest in *specific* commodities. By this I mean that you can pick and choose which markets you want to invest in. If you are bullish on oil, you can buy an oil contract. If you believe that the price of coffee will rise as changing diets sweep across industrializing nations, you can purchase a coffee contract. If you only want to profit from rising agricultural prices, you can purchase contracts on the individual agricultural commodities. You can be specific and targeted with your investment.

Take, for example, a conversation I had with a client several years ago. If you remember, 2005 was a pretty horrific hurricane season. Katrina destroyed the city of New Orleans and elsewhere, and a handful of other hurricanes tormented the East and Gulf coasts. In the aftermath of Hurricane Wilma, one of my clients from Florida called and wanted to find out about buying frozen concentrated orange juice (FCOJ) futures. His rationale was simple enough. Wilma had destroyed not only buildings but acres of orange trees. The oranges that had been ready for harvest were now lying on the ground. My client correctly surmised that because of this short-term supply disruption, FCOJ futures (trading on the New York Board of Trade) would skyrocket. Sure enough, FCOJ futures moved to a seven-year high (see Figure 4.1).

The point behind this example is that you have the ability to in-vest in specific commodity markets based on specific circumstances. Even markets that seem peculiar or lack glamour can present trading

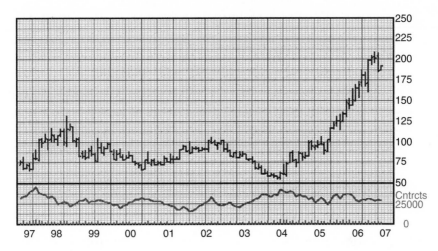

Figure 4.1 Frozen Concentrate Orange Juice (FCOJ) Nearest Futures (monthly OHLC plot)
SOURCE: Barchart.com

opportunities. And sometimes the not-so-glamorous commodities can provide investors with the most glamorous profits.

Indeed, another clear advantage of participating via commodity futures is that you can invest and profit from moves in every single tradable commodity. If we once again consider the orange juice example, my client would have been hard-pressed to find an orange juice company positively affected by that specific occurrence. It would have also been difficult (no, impossible) for him to find an orange juice ETF or a mutual fund that had a large allocation toward companies that would profit from higher orange juice prices. The same can be said for other commodities that don't necessarily have stock counterparts.

With commodity futures, you have the ability to invest in markets that seem promising. If you believe that investor demand for live cattle will pick up over the next several years, you can profit by buying live cattle futures. If you want to profit from the fact that we are anticipating a colder than expected winter in the Northeast, you can purchase heating oil futures. You get the picture.

Because you can invest in individual markets, commodity futures also provide you with the advantage of creating your own portfolio of commodities. This can actually be done a couple of different ways.

The first way is to purchase a futures contract on a specific commodity index (such as the CRB index that I mentioned in Chapter 1). This purchase will give you exposure to a basket of commodities across a number of different sectors. Alternatively, you can construct your own portfolio of some of the most undervalued commodities of each sector. For instance, if you want to purchase a couple of different commodities in the agricultural sector, a couple of different commodities in the metals sector, and a couple of different of commodities in the energy sector, you can easily do so.

It is important to keep in mind that constructing such a portfolio would depend on your risk profile, amount of capital you have to invest, and other mitigating factors. Suffice it to say, however, that commodity futures provide investors with the flexibility to participate in a wide range of commodity markets.

Commodity Stocks

Even though I have mentioned that commodity futures outperform their commodity stock counterparts by three to one, commodity stocks still can appreciate significantly during a commodity bull market. Indeed, another way that you can participate in this boom is by investing in commodity stocks. This is reaffirmed by what happened during the first stage of this bull market; some of the best-performing equities have been those that benefit from rising commodity prices.

Take, for example, the appreciation of gold and silver companies. Over the last several years, gold and silver prices have reached their highest levels in over 25 years. As a result, gold- and silver-producing companies have been able to profit from these higher prices. These profits eventually translated into higher stock prices. You can see this more clearly by looking at the Philadelphia Gold and Silver Sector Index (XAU), an index comprised of 16 gold and silver mining companies (see Figure 4.2). While it only covers a minute percentage of gold and silver stocks, it does show the general trend of these companies over the last several years.

Similarly, oil stocks have appreciated as oil prices have more than tripled over this first stage of this bull market. The Philadelphia Oil Service Sector (OSX) index tracks 15 oil-related companies (see

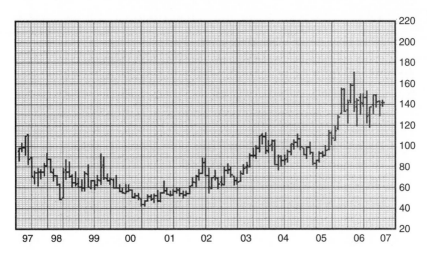

Figure 4.2 Philadelphia Stock Exchange (PHLX) Gold and Silver Index
(XAU) (Monthly)
SOURCE: Barchart.com

Figure 4.3). You can also see the appreciation of this index over the
last several years. In general, this trend is pretty much standard across
the board of all commodity stocks. The price of commodity stocks has
appreciated as their underlying commodity has increased in value.

Of course, it only makes sense that commodity-producing companies will profit from rising commodity prices. If a company is in the

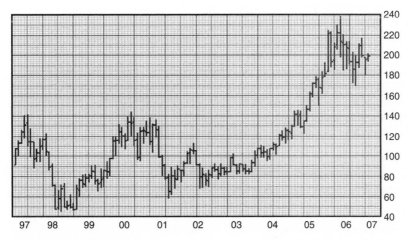

Figure 4.3 PHLX Oil Service Sector Index (OSX) (Monthly)
SOURCE: Barchart.com

business of selling a physical commodity, obviously it will make more money as the price of that commodity becomes more expensive. Another way of looking at this is that most commodity-producing companies already have a fixed cost associated with bringing their commodity to market. The cost of mining gold and bringing it to the market is the same when gold is selling at $250/ounce as it would be when gold sells at $750/ounce. The only difference is that the company is now making an additional $500/ounce. In turn, this translates into greater profits, more cash on hand, and, of course, a higher stock price.

In addition to commodity-producing companies, commodity-related companies indirectly profit from rising commodity prices. If we look at the oil sector, for example, a number of companies have been able to capitalize on higher oil prices. Higher oil prices naturally lead to oil-producing companies spending money exploring for new oil deposits. In order to explore for these deposits, they have to rely on other companies for topographical information, exploration equipment, and other goods and services. Companies that offer these types of goods and services will indirectly benefit from rising oil prices.

Consider the performance of Halliburton Company over the last several years (see Figure 4.4). It has been one of the better-performing oil stocks during this oil bull market. This comes as no surprise, as the company pretty much has its hand in a wide array of oil-related activities.

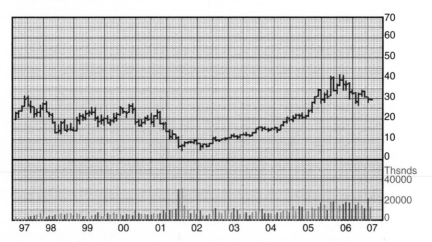

Figure 4.4   Halliburton Company (Monthly)
SOURCE: Barchart.com

It provides goods and services for oil and gas exploration as well as providing construction and maintenance for oil refineries, pipelines, and oil fields worldwide. Even though Halliburton is a commodity-related company, the price of its shares has pretty much tracked the price of oil.

The same is true for a good number of other commodity-related stocks. While these companies do not directly participate in selling the physical commodity, they indirectly profit from rising prices of the underlying commodity.

Advantages of Commodity Stocks

Depending on your investment objectives, there are also some advantages to buying commodity stocks. For one thing, it is much easier to get started. You don't have to worry about opening up a commodity futures account; you can just buy these stocks in your typical stock brokerage account. Another advantage is that you don't have to worry about any of the factors that are specific to the futures market, such as margin requirements and leverage.

Beyond the potential logistical advantages, commodity stocks also provide investors with the opportunity to profit from circumstances unrelated to the commodity bull market. For example, multiple factors can simultaneously contribute to the appreciation of a commodity stock's price. The first, of course, is the movement in the price of the underlying commodity. The other factors can be anything from management competence or incompetence, earnings, how the company performs relative to its competitors, and a variety of other unforeseen circumstances.

If you are able to find a company that is undervalued relative to its peers, you can also profit from this valuation. If you believe that the stock price of a natural gas company will rise because of better than expected earnings, you can profit from this move even if the price of natural gas remains the same.

To put this into further perspective, several smaller commodity companies have appreciated substantially after a larger company offered to buy the smaller company for a premium over the current stock price. This trend has been especially prevalent among mining companies. If you think about it, the increase in mergers and acquisitions is actually a bullish indicator for this bull market in commodities. If a company is willing to pay a substantial premium for another company five years into this bull market, the buyer obviously must feel that commodity prices still have a way to go. But regardless of the rationale behind the purchase, it is quite clear that, sometimes, holding commodity stocks might prove more profitable for investors than holding the actual commodity.

Some Disadvantages of Commodity Stocks

While unrelated factors can be beneficial to the stock price in some circumstances, in other circumstances they can negatively impact a company's stock price. Consider these examples.

- Most of a zinc mining company is located in a politically volatile country in Africa. A civil war breaks out, and the output of the mine is threatened. The stock price declines as investors fear that the worst-case scenario—mine closure—will transpire.
- A natural gas company suffers a tremendous blow as a hurricane damages or destroys 70 percent of its processing and storage facility. Even though natural gas prices skyrocket because of this supply disruption, the stock price heads in the opposite direction as investors realize the extent of the damages.
- Reports come out that a gold mining company has hedged the price of gold. As gold prices have appreciated, the company failed to fully realize profits because it spent capital hedging the downward price of gold. Investors realize that other companies might have a better quarter and proceed to sell their positions.
- A country in South America decides to nationalize its oil industry. As a result, a U.S. oil company that has substantial investments in that country suffers a huge loss. The stock price immediately declines to reflect this news.
- Scorching heat in Australia destroys a substantial amount of the wheat crop of a large producer, a publicly traded company. The supply shortage triggers a rally in wheat prices. The stock price falls, however, as investors correctly anticipate disappointing earnings.

While some of these hypothetical examples are worst-case scenarios, they can happen at any given moment and negatively impact the price of a commodity stock. Investors who choose to participate in commodity-producing stocks must also remember that in some situations, the price of the stock may decline even as the price of the underlying commodity is heading higher. Investors must be aware that other factors can come into play when investing in commodity stocks.

Investors also should be aware that just because a company classifies itself as a commodity-producing company does not necessarily mean that it will profit from rising commodity prices. In the same way that dot-com companies were "companies" in name only, scores of commodity stocks have a loose affiliation to the commodity markets. For example, dozens of mining stocks have yet to produce an ounce of gold, silver, copper, or whatever metal they claim to mine. If you invest in these companies, you should realize that you are not necessarily investing in the underlying commodity; rather you are investing in the company's ability to find that commodity. There is a big difference between having copper ore and selling it on the market and not having the copper ore and simply spending money trying to find it.

Nonetheless, most commodity stocks do present investors with another opportunity to profit from rising commodity prices. In Chapter 6 I focus on the different types of commodity companies and what you need to look for when investing in these companies.

Commodity Mutual Funds

If investing in individual companies can provide investors with a way to participate in the current commodity boom, then investing in a mutual fund that is made up of those same companies can also provide that opportunity. Thus, commodity mutual funds are another way of participating in the upward movement of commodity prices. That said, however, there are obviously several differences between investing in commodity stocks and investing in a commodity mutual fund.

Most investors are already familiar with the characteristics of mutual funds. In simple terms, a mutual fund is an investment company that invests a pool of money for investors. The decision of where the money is invested falls squarely on the shoulders of the fund manager. And in fact, this is one difference between buying commodity stocks and buying a commodity mutual fund. With stocks, individual investors are deciding what to purchase. With a mutual fund, the manager decides which stocks to purchase and the percentage to allocate to these funds.

The fact that a manager decides which commodity stocks to participate in can be a good or a bad thing. If the manager has a successful track record in selecting commodity stocks, it might make more sense to utilize his or her expertise. However, sometimes mutual funds underperform due to the poor selection of stocks by the fund manager.

Regardless of performance, investing in a commodity mutual fund involves additional fees. Typically, a sales load associated with entering into the fund (a front-end load, where you pay when you enter the fund, or a deferred sales load, where you pay when you exit) goes to the broker of record. Additionally, a yearly management fee goes to the manager of the fund. And last are the miscellaneous fees (12b-1) that typically cover expenses that are associated with running a fund. Some funds are "no-load" funds; however, most still end up charging some type of management or service fee. If you are looking at investing in a commodity mutual fund, make sure to consult the prospectus for a fee summary.

A couple of different types of commodity mutual funds are available to investors. I already mentioned the first type briefly. These funds, also called natural resource funds, invest in both commodity-producing and commodity-related stocks. Some are diversified among a wide array of companies, while others are more specific to a certain commodity sector. The mutual funds that invest in a more diversified basket of companies more closely track the direction of the general bull market in commodities.

Sector-specific mutual funds track their specific underlying commodity. Oil and gold mutual funds are two examples of sector-specific mutual funds. As you can imagine, these mutual funds fluctuate more dramatically as their underlying commodity appreciates. When the price of oil made a move from $50/barrel to $80/barrel in a relatively short period of time, oil-specific mutual funds were some of the best-performing mutual funds. Conversely, when oil prices sold off drastically in the in summer of 2006, these same funds turned into some of the worst performers for that period.

There are also mutual funds that invest in commodity futures. These funds are not as common as those that invest in commodity stocks, but they have become more prevalent over the last several years. In most cases, these funds passively track and invest in a commodity futures index. Because they invest in commodity futures, you also receive the diversifying benefits associated with the commodity futures market (i.e., noncorrelation to stocks and bonds, positive correlation with inflation, etc.)

There are also some very clear advantages to using mutual funds to participate in the commodity bull market. For instance, if you only had a limited amount of capital, it would be difficult for you to participate in a broad basket of commodity futures or a wide array of commodity stocks. You would just not have enough money to spread across the various investments. This would be especially true if you tried to replicate an actual commodity futures index. Investing a small amount of money ($5,000 to $10,000) in a diversified natural resource fund or a commodity index mutual fund could give you a broader participation in the overall commodity bull market.

Commodity Exchange-Traded Funds

Over the last several years, ETFs have taken the financial marketplace by storm. The first ETF was established in 1993 by State Street Global Advisors and was structured to track the S&P 500 index. Over time, ETFs have evolved to include a variety of investment products, including those that track a specific sector of commodity stocks, commodity index futures, and even individual commodities (such as gold, silver, and oil).

At first glance, it would seem that ETFs are just mutual funds that trade like stocks. And to an extent, this is true. When you purchase shares in an ETF, you are basically buying into an open-ended fund, a commodity pool, or a unit investment trust (UIT). These shares trade on a stock exchange and can easily be purchased through any stock brokerage account.

There are, however, some distinct advantages to purchasing ETFs. The first is that the fees associated with purchasing an ETF are much lower than the fees associated with purchasing a mutual fund. According to Morningstar, the average annual expense ratio of an ETF is

0.42 percent versus 1.3 percent for a typical mutual fund. This has to do with the fact that you are not paying a fund manager to select a portfolio of stocks for you. Instead, you are buying shares in a fund that passively tracks an already predetermined index. The other aspect is that no substantial up-front load is associated with purchasing an ETF; you only have to pay the commission to buy shares.

When it comes to trading, there is no question that commodity ETFs provide you with the ability to be much more active and nimble in the commodity marketplace. While commodity mutual funds require you to redeem your shares at the end of the day, you can buy and sell ETF shares throughout market trading hours. While commodity mutual funds allow you to profit only from the upward movement of the commodity markets, ETFs provide you with the opportunity to short and profit from downward moves. For instance, if you believed that commodities were overvalued, you could easily short the Deutsche Bank Commodity Index Tracking Fund (DBC), which tracks a diversified basket of commodity futures contracts.

Commodity ETFs that track individual and index futures also give investors the ability to participate in the futures market through a non-leveraged approach. The shares that you purchase represent a fraction of the fund that tracks the specific commodity or futures index. If the price of the commodity or index moves up by a specific percentage, your shares will also move up approximately by that percentage. With futures, the move in your account is magnified by the fact that you are using leverage. Unfortunately, only a limited number of ETFs track specific futures markets. As the bull market in commodities continues, I expect more and more such ETFs to become available.

Commodity Currencies

In an indirect way, investors can also profit from rising commodity prices by investing in the currencies of countries whose economy is largely made up of commodity exports. These currencies are often referred to as commodity currencies. Several dozen countries fall under this definition, but the term typically applies to the currencies of Australia, Canada, New Zealand, and South Africa.

Several studies have looked at the correlation between commodity prices and the currencies of countries that are heavily dependent on commodity exports. The International Monetary Fund (IMF), for example, conducted a study in which it examined the relationship between commodity currencies and commodity prices (see References at the end of the book for full information on the study). After examining the exchange rate of 58 commodity-exporting countries (of which 53 were developing economies), the IMF concluded:

> Our study found evidence in support of the co-movement of national exchange rates and real commodity prices in a group of commodity exporting countries. For these commodity currency countries, the world price of their commodity exports has a stable and important effect on their real exchange rate.

Indeed, it should come as no surprise that commodity currencies are positively influenced by rising commodity prices. As the demand for commodities continues to grow, the economies that export these commodities will grow. In turn, their currencies should appreciate accordingly. Take a look at the performance of the Canadian dollar during the first stage of this bull market (see Figure 4.5). Since its lows in 2002,

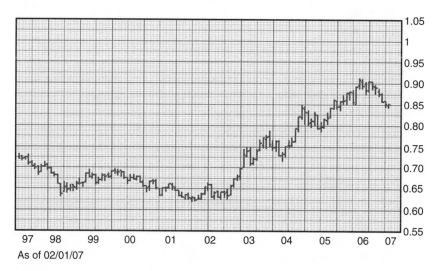

As of 02/01/07

Figure 4.5 Canadian Dollar Performance (Monthly)
SOURCE: Barchart.com

the Canadian dollar has pretty much tracked the upward trend of the commodity market.

The Canadian economy relies heavily on commodity exports. So much so that when you combine all the exports from the commodity sector (mining, energy, agriculture, forestry, etc.), the raw materials industry accounts for 40 percent of Canada's yearly exports. Equally as important is that over the last several years, the commodity sector has contributed toward a $58 billion surplus. These factors obviously bode well for the Canadian currency. And this is reflected in the fact that it has appreciated significantly over the past several years.

The same can be said for the other commodity currencies. The Australian dollar, for example, has been propped up higher due to the fact that its economy and currency are strongly influenced by commodity prices. Australia is the world's third largest gold producer, a major grain exporter, and the world's largest coal exporter. It also doesn't hurt that the country is in close proximity to China and other industrializing Asian economies. Hence, the Australian dollar has appreciated over 35 percent since the start of this bull market.

Of course, other factors can affect the exchange rate of these countries. However, it is quite clear that rising commodity prices can have a positive affect on the appreciation of commodity currencies. You can indirectly profit either by buying futures contracts on the currencies or by investing in cash accounts that hold these currencies.

Deciding What's Right for You

As you can see, quite a few different investment vehicles allow you to participate and profit from this long-term commodity boom. Some investment vehicles allow you to participate in a direct manner, while others allow you to participate in a more indirect and roundabout way.

Which investment vehicles should you use to profit from this long-term commodity boom? Should you allocate your funds to only one investment vehicle? Or should you consider spreading your investment among several different ones?

Unfortunately, I cannot answer this question for every single reader. Every investor differs in investment objectives and goals. For instance, if you like to be more hands-on with your investments, participating via individual futures contracts or actual stocks might be the best way for you to go. If, however, you are more concerned with having an allocation to a broad basket of commodities and could care less about hands-on participation, investing in commodity mutual funds or commodity index ETFs might best meet your needs.

Before deciding on what is right for you, I suggest that you review the various ways that you can participate in this bull market. Then ask yourself these questions:

- What are your investment goals? Do you care more about diversification, or are you more interested in profiting from record commodity prices?
- How active do you want to be in the investment decisions? Do you want to decide which specific commodity markets to enter, or are you okay with letting a fund manager decide?
- Do you want to participate directly or indirectly in the commodity bull market?
- Can you participate in all of these investment vehicles? In other words, do you have a commodity brokerage account or the funds necessary to set up an account?
- Does your 401k allow you to participate in individual stocks?

Consulting an investment professional who readily agrees with the long-term bull market in commodities might be a good way to figure out whether you should invest in futures, stocks, mutual funds, ETFs, or all of the above. Remember, if the advisor scoffs at the idea that we are in a long-term commodity bull market, there is a good chance that he or she will steer you away from any commodity-related investment. My advice is to find another advisor. Or you can always hand him or her a copy of this book.

Conclusion

When you consider the vastness and reach of the commodity markets, it makes perfect sense that there are many different ways to profit from rising commodity prices. The increased consumption of raw materials by industrializing economies will not only benefit those who own the phys-ical commodities (or futures); it will also favorably impact shareholders of commodity companies, investors who own commodity mutual funds or ETFs, and even those whose portfolios have an allocation to commodity currencies.

The main difference among the investment vehicles is how they benefit from rising prices. Besides that, deciding on which investment vehicle or vehicles to use during this commodity bull market depends on what you are trying to accomplish. Subsequent chapters shed additional clarity on this subject.

Chapter 5

Participating Through Futures

*The price of a commodity will never go to zero. When you invest in
commodities futures, you're not buying a piece of paper that says you
own an intangible piece of company that can go bankrupt.*

—Jim Rogers

W hen it comes to participating in the commodity futures
market, it is important to differentiate among the different
commodity sectors as well as among the individual markets
that make up those sectors. Up to this point, our discussion about the
bull market in commodities has been more general. The premise was
simply that we are in a long-term commodity boom, and the supply and
demand constraints facing the various commodity markets will continue
to push the price of commodities higher.

While this statement is true and to the point, it fails to address the
reality that the overall commodity futures market is made up of various
markets that do not necessarily move in the same direction. You cannot
assume that just because we are in a commodity boom, a certain sector

will appreciate during a specific time period. There will be times when certain commodity sectors lead while others lag.

This makes perfect sense. In the same way that different stock market sectors react differently in varying market conditions, the different commodity futures markets will appreciate during different times of this commodity bull market. Some of these factors might be interrelated in a broader sense, but they typically vary in how they impact specific commodity sectors and markets. Take, for example, the demand for industrial metals from China. As I have pointed out, demand for copper, nickel, aluminum, and other industrial metals is increasing exponentially as China continues to transform its agrarian economy into an industrial powerhouse. Because of this, industrial metals have appreciated greatly and will continue to appreciate for the next several years.

But what about the price of coffee? Will the demand for these metals also have an immediate and positive impact on the price of coffee? Of course not. Nor will a bullish report on coffee have a positive impact on the copper futures market. Different factors will affect different markets and sectors. Thus, distinguishing among the futures markets is important if you are looking to profit from this bull market.

In this chapter I look at the different futures sectors that make up this commodity bull market and at some of the markets that make up these sectors. Some of these markets I discuss in more detail, while others I only briefly touch on. Note also that there are many more commodity futures markets that I do not have space to discuss. The purpose of this chapter is to introduce you to the variety of commodity futures markets, elaborate on some of their key characteristics, and reaffirm some of the fundamental factors discussed previously.

Different Commodity Futures Sectors

There are many different ways in which you can dissect and look at the commodity futures markets. One way is to distinguish between hard and soft commodities. Hard commodities are those that are finite in nature (such as metals and energy), while soft commodities are those that are renewable in nature (such as agriculture and softs). Another way would be to clump them into groups, such as precious metals, industrial metals, industrial materials, food products, livestock, and so on. Quite honestly, you can group them any way you like. One of the more common ways, however, is to break them up across five commodity sectors:

1. Energy futures
2. Grains futures
3. Meats futures
4. Softs futures
5. Metals futures

On futures Web sites, quotes generally are grouped in these sectors. For instance, the price of wheat would be displayed under the grains sector alongside other agricultural commodities. The price of the December futures contract on light crude oil would be listed under the energy sector.

Within these sectors are the actual commodities that you can trade. However, just because commodity futures markets are grouped together in one sector does not mean that they will move in the same direction. This is why it is also important to look at the individual factors that affect the different futures markets.

Selecting Markets

Furthermore, it is important to know that you do not have to participate in every single futures market to participate fully in this commodity bull market. One of the first things that you will notice is that there are quite a few commodity futures markets. Some of these markets are fairly obvious (gold, oil, and corn); others (e.g., milk, bean meal, and flaxseed oil) are obscure to the average commodity investor. Should you even consider investing in these commodities? How will you become knowledgeable on the supply and demand factors that affect their prices?

The answer is that you don't have to participate or become knowledgeable in every single commodity futures market. You can if you like, but it makes more sense to know more about a diversified group of commodities than to know a little bit about every single commodity futures market. Even I don't know the detailed supply and demand fundamentals behind every single tradable commodity. If you wanted to know the prospects of flaxseed oil, I would probably refer you to someone else.

Nonetheless, it is important to know the general sectors and several markets within those sectors that will likely profit from this commodity boom. Focusing on the five sectors just mentioned will not only help organizationally, but it will also allow you to view the long-term bull market in commodities a little bit more closely.

For instance, various sectors will perform well throughout different stages of this commodity boom. In the boom's first stage, there was a greater focus on industrialization and the need for basic materials. Consequently, the metals and energy sectors would stand to appreciate the most from this demand. And sure enough, those two sectors have been the best-performing ones of this bull market.

This closer look at the commodity bull market will also allow you to focus on value plays within each sector and which sectors might be undervalued during various stages. Additionally, you can choose to spread your investments across the different sectors or simply invest in sectors you feel are the most undervalued. If you do spread your investments across different sectors, you will probably have a more diversified approach to the various stages of this commodity boom.

Different Futures Exchanges

Another thing that you will notice about the futures markets is that there are several commodity exchanges on which you can buy and sell futures contracts. In some cases, certain futures contracts trade on only one exchange. If you wanted to participate in that commodity, then you would have to transact on that exchange. However, some futures contracts trade on multiple exchanges. Gold futures, for example, trade on the Chicago Board of Trade, the New York Mercantile Exchange, the London Metals Exchange, the Tokyo Commodity Exchange, and the Sydney Futures Exchange.

As I mentioned earlier in the book, it does not really matter which exchange you trade on. More than anything, it will be easier if you pick an exchange that is in your country or region, because trading hours of the exchanges are different, contract specifications can be different, and in most cases the currency in which the commodities trade is also different. Most of the futures markets trade on U.S. exchanges.

Another thing that I want to point out is that a good number of factors can affect a futures market on a short- and intermediate-term basis. Reports of increasing supply in a market, a potential discovery of a hard commodity, and a temporary slowdown of the Chinese economy are just a few examples that could alter the short-term outlook of some of these markets. However, the long-term outlook for these markets and sectors will typically remain positive. Remember that the factors I discuss are only a part of the bigger picture when it comes to the direction of these markets. More than anything else, I hope to show how commodity futures relate to this long-term commodity boom and how the futures market is an integral part of our daily lives.

Energy Futures

The energy futures sector is a vital component of this commodity bull market, because it is literally the engine behind industrialization and consumer consumption. If you look at the growth that has occurred in China, for example, none of that would have happened without some type of energy source. For instance, in order for a plot of farmland to be transformed into a bustling factory or city, you need some type of energy to power the machinery to build the roads and buildings, you need some form of fuel to transport the materials and equipment to the location, and you need some type of energy to keep it all running once it has all been built.

The same can be said for the increase in consumer consumption. If all of a sudden there is an increase in demand for a certain consumer product, more energy is needed to build that product. If that product happens to be a car or an electrical appliance, even more energy is needed to keep it running.

The bottom line is that energy demand has increased over the last several years. Given the fact that we are still in the early to middle stages of industrialization, I would expect this demand to continue to increase. Since there are different types of energy sources, there are also different energy futures markets. Some of the more popular and actively traded energy futures markets are:

- Crude oil futures
- Natural gas futures
- Unleaded gasoline futures

- Heating oil futures
- Coal futures

Crude Oil Futures

The crude oil futures market is without question the bedrock of the energy sector. Not only is crude oil the main component of gasoline, heating oil, and a variety of other petrochemicals, but it also accounts for approximately 40 percent of the world's energy supply.

Crude oils differ based on gravity, location, and sulfur content. Oil containing more than 0.5 percent sulfur by weight is called sour crude. Oil containing less than 0.5 percent sulfer is referred to as sweet crude. As discussed earlier, the quality and delivery location of the commodity should be standardized for each futures contract. Consequently, different types of crude oil contracts trade in the futures market.

Brent crude oil, for example, is a light sweet crude oil that hails from the North Sea. As a result, it is traded in London and is also recognized as the world benchmark when it comes to oil prices. In comparison, oil that is from the United States is referred to as West Texas Intermediate (WTI) crude. More commonly, this is the light, sweet crude that trades on the New York Mercantile Exchange (NYMEX). In the United States, when the price of crude oil is quoted, WTI crude is being referred to.

The long-term outlook for crude oil is centered on the concept discussed in Chapter 1: supply and demand. There are two schools of thought regarding the crude oil supply. The first camp believes that there is enough crude oil to meet the world's energy needs. Newfound technology will allow for the discovery of new deposits, the extraction of previously untapped oil sources (such as oil sands), and even the recycling of crude oil. Although some additional deposits might be discovered, this hopeful outlook fails to address the fact that there is a finite amount of fossil fuel in Earth's crust. The world's greatest technological advance will not be able to find oil when there is no oil to be found.

The second camp, of which I am a part, believes that crude oil output is on the decline due to its finite nature. While there are many theories and postulations behind crude oil decline, none is more famous than the peak oil theory, which was first presented to the American

Petroleum Institute by geophysicist Marion King Hubbert in 1956. The gist of the theory is that Earth's production of oil will peak at some point in time; after the peak, oil production will permanently decline. In his paper, Hubbert also predicted that oil production in the United States would peak in between 1965 and 1970 and that worldwide production would peak fifty years or so later.

Interestingly enough, U.S. oil production did peak in 1971. There is still a debate, however, on whether a peak in global production has occurred. Regardless of when exactly we will see this peak, it is quite clear that supply of crude oil is declining in a terminal manner. Besides the United States, crude oil production has peaked in over 50 oil-producing countries. I suspect that this number is even greater, but some of the larger oil-producing nations have not yet admitted the truth. In any case, the downward trend seems to be accelerating just as global demand is starting to pick up.

Many disagree with the grim crude oil supply outlook, but most agree that the demand for crude oil has increased incrementally over the last several years. In its *International Energy Outlook Report*, the Energy Information Administration (EIA) projected that world energy demand will grow from 80 million barrels per day in 2003, to 98 million barrels in 2015, to 118 million barrels per day in 2030. Not surprisingly, China, India, and other developing Asian economies account for 43 percent of the growth over this period.

The demand for crude oil once again goes back to the greatest commodity boom of our generation. Crude oil consumption will continue to increase as these economies continue to grow and consumers continue to consume. That said, speculation nevertheless does enter the crude oil futures market. Take, for instance, the continued geopolitical tensions in the Middle East. Whenever some news breaks that can have an impact on oil supply, crude oil futures markets generally respond by moving higher. Speculation also enters the picture as some investors try to chase profits. We saw this scenario when the price of oil had a quick move up to $80/barrel in 2006.

However, it is shortsighted to assume that the multiyear move that has occurred in crude oil futures was a result of speculation. The bulk of the move has been a result of simple fundamental factors. Whereas in the past, most of the oil consumption was centered in the United States and other developed economies, China and others have now entered the race for the last drop of crude oil supply.

Going forward, I see the price of crude oil reaching $150 a barrel. While this number might seem optimistic to some, remember that, on an inflation-adjusted basis, the price of oil has still not reached its all-time high. That all-time high, closer to $100/barrel, occurred in 1980. Since then we have much less supply and greater demand. Take a look at some of the contract specifications for crude oil futures.

Key Contract Specifications for Crude Oil Futures
1 Contract: 1,000 barrels of oil or 42,000 gallons
Prices Quoted: U.S. dollars and cents per barrel
Trading Symbol: CL
Exchange: NYMEX
Trading Months: Monthly for the current year and 5 years out

TIP
Don't let the price determine your investment decisions. Just because a commodity has doubled in price does not necessarily mean it's overvalued. Look at the driving factors behind the move and remember that the nominal price is different from the real (inflation-adjusted) price.

Natural Gas Futures

Like crude oil, natural gas futures trade on the NYMEX. The most liquid contract is called Henry Hub natural gas; the contract is based on the delivery of the gas at the Henry Hub facility in Louisiana.

As an energy source, natural gas is widely popular in the United States. In fact, natural gas makes up 25 percent of the overall energy consumption in this country. One reason is that natural gas is quite inexpensive compared to other energy sources. Furthermore, over the last few decades, technological and infrastructure advances have enabled natural gas to be transported to a larger population.

Natural gas serves as a fuel for natural-gas-powered vehicles and to generate electricity for residential and industrial sectors. As an example, more than half of the homes in the United States use natural gas for heat and/or cooling. Thus, the price of natural gas often spikes when we have extreme weather conditions in either direction. On the flip side, prices often decline during mild seasonal temperatures.

The global demand outlook for natural gas is also strong. According to the EIA, natural gas consumption will increase at a much faster rate than crude oil over the next 25 years. China, India, and other emerging economies will lead the percentage increase in natural gas. Today the United States and other developed countries are the primary users of natural gas because that they already have an established infrastructure. However, as developing countries begin to build their own natural gas pipelines and facilities, this increase in demand should push natural gas futures prices to new highs over the next several years.

The natural gas market is extremely volatile. Over the last several years there has been a wide fluctuation in the price of natural gas futures. Take a look at Figure 5.1. As you can see, during this commodity boom the price has moved from as low as $2 in 2001–2002 to as high as $14 in 2005 and back down to $4 in 2006. One of the reasons for this fluctuation is due to the fact that natural gas is a much more weather-related commodity than crude oil. In 2005, for instance, we had a strong hurricane season and cold winter. In 2006 the price of natural gas

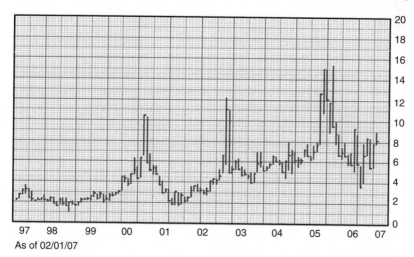

Figure 5.1 Natural Gas Chart (Monthly)
SOURCE: Barchart.com

declined in the midst of a mild early winter and a relatively uneventful hurricane season.

Key Contract Specifications for Natural Gas Futures
1 Contract: 10,000 million British thermal units (mmBtu)
Prices Quoted: U.S. dollars and cents per mmBtu
Trading Symbol: NG
Exchange: NYMEX
Trading Months: Monthly for the current year and 5 years out

Unleaded Gasoline Futures

As I stated earlier, gasoline is the by-product of refined crude oil. Not surprisingly, gasoline futures prices often move in similar directions to crude oil prices. When the price of oil futures climbed to over $80/barrel, unleaded gasoline futures traded at over $2.30/gallon. When tensions in the Middle East affect crude oil prices, unleaded gasoline futures respond in the same manner.

Other factors, however, can also contribute to the price of unleaded gasoline futures. Take, for example, a couple of different scenarios that affected the price of gasoline futures over the last couple of years. In September 2005 gasoline futures spiked higher as Hurricane Katrina ravaged the Gulf Coast. Even though gasoline futures are traded primarily in the New York Harbor area, the major refining center is located on the Gulf Coast. As you can imagine, Katrina negatively impacted these refining centers, which led to a shortage of production, which tightened the supply of unleaded gasoline on the market. Then in 2006, unleaded gas futures headed higher as gasoline refiners were forced to switch out the environmentally harmful MTBE additive with ethanol.

By and large, gasoline futures appreciate along with the general crude oil fundamentals.

Key Contract Specification for Unleaded Gasoline Futures
1 Contract: 42,000 gallons or 1,000 barrels
Prices Quoted: U.S. dollars and cents per gallon
Trading Symbol: HU
Exchange: NYMEX
Trading Months: 12 consecutive months

Heating Oil Futures

After gasoline, heating oil accounts for the second largest amount of crude oil used. Consequently, I also believe that heating oil futures will move up as crude oil futures move higher. As the term "heating oil" (also known as No. 2 oil) indicates, it is used primarily as fuel to heat homes. Most of the heating oil customers are located primarily in the Northeast, where homes have basements that can accommodate the storage of heating oil.

Historically, heating oil futures rise when the winter months come along. Similar to natural gas, this is a result of the increased demand by residents to heat their homes. Typically heating oil futures appreciate drastically during extremely cold winters in the Northeast. Conversely, if there is limited seasonal demand due to milder weather, heating oil prices also decline.

Key Contract Specifications for Heating Oil Futures
1 Contract: 42,000 gallons or 1,000 barrels
Prices Quoted: U.S. dollars and cents per gallon
Trading Symbol: HO
Exchange: NYMEX
Trading Months: 18 consecutive months

TIP
Expand your focus. Recognize that we are living in a changing world. Having a U.S.-centric focus in the global marketplace limits where you will invest or what you think has value.

Coal Futures

Even though coal might seem archaic to some, it still powers a large part of the world. By burning the coal at a power plant, steam is created; the steam is then transferred through a turbine to produce electricity. Thus, if the demand for electricity increases, the demand for coal will increase, as well.

In the United States, coal accounts for greater than half of the electricity output. In India, coal consumption is growing at a record pace, even though it already accounts for two-thirds of the country's overall energy consumption. As industrialization and consumer demand continues to grow, I expect the demand for coal to increase, as well. Like oil, it takes several million years for coal to form. In other words, this is another case of demand being at odds with finite supply.

Central Appalachian coal futures trade on the NYMEX. As you probably have already noticed, a good many futures contracts are named after the region of output; with coal, the primary region in the United States is in the Appalachian Mountain area.

Key Contract Specifications for Coal Futures
Trading Unit: 1 contract = 1,550 tons of coal
Prices Quoted: U.S. dollars and cents per ton
Trading Symbol: QL
Exchange: NYMEX
Trading Months: Every month to 3 years out

Grains Futures

The grains sector can be viewed as the agricultural or food sector of the commodity futures market. In comparison to the metals and energy sectors, the grains sector has yet to see its best days of appreciation. Of course, it is logical that grains typically will appreciate in the latter part of the commodity bull market. Whereas energy and metal commodities typically benefit from industrial demand, food commodities will benefit from the growth in the standard of living of the consumer. When the average Chinese citizen has a lot more money to spend, he or she likely will spend part of it to spice up a previously mundane diet.

In China, there has already been a dramatic shift in diet. It is estimated that in the 1960s, meat consumption made up only 3.9 percent of the average daily calorie intake. The greater majority of the diet consisted of rice, wheat, or potatoes. Over the last 40-plus years, not only has the average daily caloric intake increased, but the diet is also more diverse.

Yet, in comparison to western economies, China has still a way to go when it comes to food intake and trends.

Even so, in terms of actual consumption, China is the world's top consumer of wheat, rice, and soybeans. In addition, even as China's production of grains has increased over the last several years, it has not been enough to cover domestic demand. China used to be a net exporter of grains, but now it is a net importer of most grains. Indeed, this transition highlights a couple of factors. Not only will the increased demand on the world supply push prices higher, but this increased demand also reaffirms the voracious agricultural appetite of the Chinese consumer.

Other fundamental factors also will positively affect the grains sector over the life of this bull market. First, the sheer fact that the world's population is growing is bullish for most food commodities. A simple way of looking at this is that there will be substantially more mouths to feed. While the current grains supply might be enough for the current population, it will not be enough to keep up with the rapid growth of the human race.

The second factor has to do with the supply constraints of the grains markets. Intuitively, one would imagine that if there was an increase in the demand for grains, more acres would be planted to meet the demand. However, as I have pointed out, one of the negative impacts of industrialization is that farmland becomes less available with the creation of cities and industrial sectors. In addition, some grains (e.g., corn and soybeans) are used for energy alternatives. This demand from the energy sector will obviously take away from the food supply.

The long-term supply and demand factors that are affecting the grains futures sector as a whole also translate down to the individual markets. Some of the futures markets in the grains sector that stand to benefit from these food trends (as well as other factors) are wheat, corn, and soybean futures.

Wheat Futures

You can buy or sell wheat futures contracts on the Kansas City Board of Trade, Minneapolis Grain Exchange, and Chicago Board of Trade (CBOT). Once again, the difference among the contracts is based on type and specifications. KC Wheat is also known as hard red winter wheat; Minneapolis Wheat is known as hard red spring wheat; and Chicago Wheat is the soft red winter type. However, the most actively traded futures contract is CBOT wheat.

Wheat is used primarily in three different areas. The most obvious and most popular is for food. The refined product of wheat is flour, which is used in everything from breads to cereal to baked goods. The second use is as a feed product for animals, and the third use is as an industrial additive.

Key Contract Specifications for Wheat Futures
Trading Unit: 1 contract = 5,000 bushels
Prices Quoted: U.S. cents and quarter cents per bushel
Trading Symbol: W
Exchange: CBOT
Trading Months: March, May, July, September, December

Corn Futures

Although it may come as a surprise to some investors, the greatest use of corn is as a feed for poultry, hogs, and cattle. However, corn is also used extensively as a food product for humans. Besides the always tasty corn on the cob, corn by-products can be found in hundreds of different food items, such as cornstarch, sweeteners, salad dressings, cereals, and snack foods.

In addition, corn by-products are found in such non–food-related products as toothpaste, household cleaners, and cardboard. Most recently, corn has received a lot of attention because of the demand for it as an energy source. In the Midwest, for instance, a large number of farmers have taken advantage of the ethanol boom and planted more corn.

Key Contract Specifications for Corn Futures
Trading Unit: 1 contract = 5,000 bushels
Prices Quoted: U.S. cents and quarter cents per bushel
Trading Symbol: C
Exchange: CBOT
Trading Months: March, May, July, September, December

Soybean Futures

The United States produces 40 percent of the world's soybean crop and is a great exporter of soybeans to the other parts of the world. The biggest consumer of soybeans is China. Like most of the other agricultural crops already mentioned, soybeans are used as a food product, a feed product, and an industrial product. Like corn, soybeans can also be used as an energy source.

There are several different futures contracts associated with soybeans. You can buy futures contracts on soybeans, soybean meal, soybean oil. This variety of different types of soybean futures contracts relates to the makeup and benefits of the futures market. Since there are a wide variety of uses for soybeans, many manufacturers are looking at hedging their costs. A food manufacturer that primarily uses soybean oil generally will want to transact in the soybean oil futures market. Another manufacturer might only need to use soybean meal. In general, the manufactures want to focus on the actual products that they use. As a result, futures markets were established to facilitate these diverse needs.

Although in some situations the different soybean futures markets trade differently from each other, typically the long-term moves of the soybean futures soybean oil futures, and soybean meal futures are the same.

Key Contract Specifications for Soybean Futures
Trading Unit: 1 contract = 5,000 bushels
Prices Quoted: U.S. cents per bushel
Trading Symbol: S
Exchange: CBOT
Trading Months: January, March, May, July, August, September, November

Meats Futures

The change in diets that will occur in the next several years will result in an increased demand for more expensive food commodities. Thus, in this bull market environment, the meats tend to do very well. Take a look at Figure 5.2.

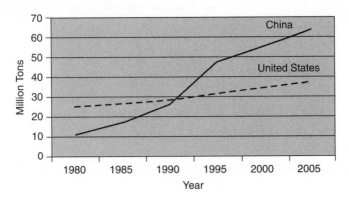

Figure 5.2   Meat Consumption in China and the United States, 1980 to 2005
SOURCE: U.S. Department of Agriculture

As you can see, meat consumption in China has risen exponentially over the last 25 years. You will also notice that China has overtaken the United States in terms of meat consumption. This of course, has to do with China's much larger population. This increased meat consumption trend will likely continue for the next decade.

The meats sector also can be affected by various trends not related to the general bull market in commodities. However, one thing is certain: If the long-term trend of grains is up, the cost to feed cattle, pigs, and poultry will also rise. As a result, you can also expect rising prices in this commodity sector.

Besides eggs, milk, and butter, some of the markets that make up the meats futures sector are live cattle, feeder cattle, and lean hogs.

Live Cattle Futures

Live cattle futures are contracts on cattle that are already mature and ready for slaughter. In other words, when you take delivery of live cattle, you are pretty much taking delivery of the meat. While live cattle futures were established as a risk management tool for ranchers and those in the meat industry, they also have provided opportunity for speculators to invest. For example, speculators who were short live cattle futures during the mad cow disease scare would have taken advantage of the decline of cattle prices because the demand for beef had declined.

Live cattle futures were the first nonstorable commodity traded; they were introduced by the Chicago Mercantile Exchange in 1964. Previously, all other traded commodities had to be stored at one location or another. Since that time, we have seen multiple futures contracts on nonstorable commodities.

Key Contract Specifications for Live Cattle Futures
Trading Unit: 1 contract = 40,000 pounds of cattle
Prices Quoted: U.S. cents per pound
Trading Symbol: LC
Exchange: CME
Trading Months: February, April, June, August, October, December

Feeder Cattle Futures

In contrast to live cattle, feeder cattle are younger cattle that are not quite ready for slaughter. Feeder cattle typically weigh anywhere from 650 to 849 pounds. Feeder cattle are grown until they reach a certain size, then they are shipped to feedlots, where they are fattened up for slaughter. Stated another way, feeder cattle mature into live cattle.

Beyond the demand for meat, another factor that might influence both feeder and live cattle futures is the price of feed. Feeder cattle feed is generally corn, wheat, or soybean meal. As you can imagine, if the price of feed increases, the cost of raising the cattle will also increase. In the short term, however, the opposite is likely to occur. Since the price of feed keeps on rising, ranchers may get out of the business and start selling their cattle. This will lead to an additional supply of cattle on the market and a short-term price decline. This scenario played out in the fall of 2006, when corn prices had a vicious rally toward the upside and feeder cattle futures declined in response to the higher prices.

Key Contract Specifications for Feeder Cattle Futures
Trading Unit: 1 contract = 50,000 pounds of cattle
Prices Quoted: U.S. cents per pound
Trading Symbol: FC
Exchange: CME
Trading Months: January, March, April, May, August, September, October, November

Lean Hogs Futures

Lean hogs futures are similar to the cattle futures in that they are a hedging tool for those involved in the meat industry. The contracts trade on the Chicago Mercantile Exchange and typically fluctuate on some of the similar demand factors associated with the other meats. Change of diets, diet fads, and other consumer-driven factors also can have an effect on the price of lean hogs futures.

For example, in late 2003 and early 2004, lean hogs futures appreciated by more than 35 percent. The reason for this appreciation was largely due to a change in diet as consumers shifted from beef because of news of mad cow disease.

Key Contract Specifications for Lean Hogs Futures
Trading Unit: 1 contract = 40,000 pounds
Prices Quoted: U.S. cents per pound
Trading Symbol: LN
Exchange: CME
Trading Months: February, April, May, June, July, August, October, December

Softs Futures

During the 1970s bull market in commodities, the softs futures sector experienced explosive growth. I believe that the same scenario will play out in the latter stages of this commodity boom. The softs futures sector is comprised of a diverse mix of commodities. On one end, you have "tropical commodities," such as coffee, sugar, cocoa, and orange juice. On the other end, you have "fiber" commodities, such as cotton and lumber.

Because this sector is so diverse, the fundamental factors that affect it vary widely. Sugar, for instance, can fall in both the food and energy (ethanol) category. Coffee, cocoa, and orange juice fall under the food category, but lumber and cotton do not. In short, when you look at the softs futures sector, make sure to focus on market-by-market fundamentals.

Some of the more popular softs futures markets include:

- Cotton futures
- Coffee futures
- Sugar futures

Cotton Futures

Cotton futures have been trading in New York since the late 1800s. Historically, cotton has always been a valuable commodity because of its widespread use. As a commodity, cotton is a soft fiber that is used mostly in clothing and textiles. Not surprisingly, the United States is the world's largest consumer of cotton. When it comes to production, China, the United States, and India are the world's largest producers.

One of the interesting characteristics of cotton is that it can grow in a wide range of areas. That is why cotton production can be found across multiple continents. There are, however, differences in the type of cotton. Coarse cotton is used primarily for denimlike material, while premium cotton is used in softer fabrics.

Over the last several years, cotton consumption has increased heavily, especially in emerging economies. Chinese cotton consumption has increased from 6 million tons to 9.7 million tons over a three-year period from 2002 to 2005. In India, cotton consumption increased by over 14.5 percent during this first stage of this bull market.

Key Cotton Futures Specifications
Trading Unit: 1 contract = 50,000 pounds
Prices Quoted: U.S. cents and hundredths of cent per pound
Trading Symbol: CT
Exchange: NYBOT
Trading Months: Current month plus one or more of the next 23 succeeding months. Active trading months: March, May, July, October, December

Coffee Futures

Even though coffee as a beverage has been around since the late ninth century, its popularity has grown significantly over the last 20 years. You need only to walk around major cities to see the extent of coffee growth and consumption in the United States.

While consumption is great in developed economies, it is still in the early stages of most developing economies. As these economies continue to undergo tremendous growth in terms of wealth creation, I expect that coffee demand will increase steadily. Already China is starting to experience an incremental demand. Coffee demand is expected to grow from 40,000 to 50,000 metric tons in 2006 to a projected 60,000 to 70,000 metric tons in 2007. And even that amount is much less than per capita consumption of other developed economies.

In India, a predominantly tea-drinking country, coffee consumption is also increasing. From 1980 to 2000, India consumed approximately 60,000 metric tons every year. According to the Indian Coffee Board, over the last five years, consumption has grown to over 80,000 metric tons per year and is expected to grow to 100,000 metric tons by 2009.

Key Coffee Futures Specifications
Trading Unit: 1 contract = 37,500 pounds
Prices Quoted: U.S. cents per pound
Trading Symbol: KC
Exchange: NYBOT
Trading Months: March, May, July, September, December

Sugar Futures

Two types of sugar futures contracts trade on the New York Board of Trade: Sugar #11 and Sugar #13. The more actively traded sugar contract is Sugar #11.

Sugar is produced in over 120 countries and consumed in literally every country in the world. Most sugar produced in a country (about 70 percent) is consumed in that country; the remaining amount is traded internationally. In terms of consumption per country, India and China are the world's top consumers of sugar. In terms of per capita consumption, there is still room for growth (see Figure 5.3). The reason has to do with the fact that sugar is a type of commodity that experiences increased consumption demand as discretionary spending increases. In other words, when citizens of developing nations have more money to

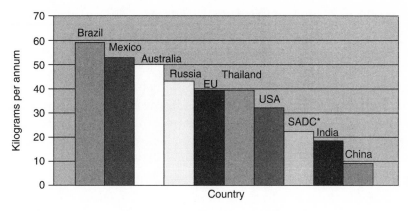

Figure 5.3 Per Capita Sugar Consumption, 2005 to 2006
*Southern African Development Community

spend on food, they will likely spend some of that money on nonstaple foods (sweets, processed foods, and beverages).

If you notice, Brazil consumes the most amount of sugar per capita, for a couple of reasons. First, Brazil does consume a good amount of sugar as a food product, but it also uses a tremendous amount of sugar as fuel. Indeed, the demand for sugar-based ethanol has increased as the need for a cheaper and more environmentally friendly fuel alternative has increased. Sweden and Japan, which have passed several initiatives to comply with emissions standards (e.g., the Kyoto Protocol), have increased their sugar-based ethanol imports.

As a result of this increased demand over the last several years, many sugar-producing countries (Brazil, Thailand, Australia, etc.) are set to expand their sugar production. While this will bring added supply on the market, it remains to be seen if it will have an effect on the supply deficit that has occurred in the sugar markets over the last several years.

Key Sugar Futures Specifications
Trading Unit: 1 contract = 112,000 pounds
Prices Quoted: U.S. cents per pound
Trading Symbol: SB
Exchange: NYBOT
Trading Months: March, May, July, October

Metals Futures

All across the board, the metals futures sector has been one of the best-performing sectors of this bull market in commodities. Within this sector are a wide array of metals that typically fall into one of two categories. The precious metals category is made up of metals that are used for jewelry or denote some type of monetary worth. The industrial metals category is made up of metals that are used for industrial purposes.

When it comes to the current commodity boom, there seems to be no end in sight for the demand for metals. Just as the energy sector is needed to power industrialization, industrial metals are needed to provide the foundation for the growth. From copper pipes to aluminum awnings to steel frames, the metals are a vital cog in the industrialization that is taking place in one-third of the world. Given the fact that this process is not yet complete, I believe that there will be continued demand for the irreplaceable metals sector.

Some of the futures markets that make up this sector are:

- Copper futures
- Platinum futures
- Palladium futures
- Gold futures
- Silver futures

Copper Futures

Copper is one of the world's most versatile metals. Its malleability, conductivity, and durability make copper useful for a wide range of industries and products. For instance, if you have ever walked into a hardware store, you will find copper plumbing, copper wiring, copper pipes, copper fixtures, and a slew of other copper products. Additionally, copper can be found in cars, in telecommunications equipment, and even in MP3 players.

Copper futures trade on several worldwide exchanges. In the United States, however, copper futures trade on the Commodity Exchange (COMEX) which is a division of the New York Mercantile Exchange. Since there are multiple grades of copper, the futures contracts that trade on the COMEX are distinguished as high-grade copper.

The first stage of this commodity bull market has provided copper with favorable results. The price of copper has appreciated by over 200 percent since its lows in 2001. During this same time period, China has increased its copper consumption by over 87 percent. If you have read this far, it should not come as a surprise that a good majority of the copper demand has come from the industrializing countries. With every building that is erected, a certain amount of copper is required.

I do not think that the demand for copper will stall anytime soon. The need for and uses of copper are too wide and too diverse. Various industries use copper, and industrializing economies need it if they want to continue their path toward a modern economy.

In addition to the continued demand for copper, there has been an ever-increasing worry about its supply. All over the globe, copper inventories are down, and the last several years have resulted in deficits in the copper market. In other words, there was more demand for copper than was mined in the year. As a result, copper inventories were ravaged to fill the gap.

I do not believe, however, that current inventories will be able to fill the gap between supply and demand. The fact that there has not been a major copper mine discovery in close to 100 years also makes the supply case even more worrisome. Additionally, Chile, the world's largest producer of copper, is already starting to see a decline in production. All of these factors combined make me believe that we are still in the first half of a copper bull market.

With that said, I do want to highlight the speculative movements that have occurred in the copper markets over the last several years. The meteoric rise in copper prices, and the subsequent correction, is an example of how speculation often enters the commodity markets. In other words, while the demand for copper was warranted, the exponential move was not. Many speculators entered the copper markets strictly to chase returns. As a result, the commodity markets often got ahead of themselves.

Copper Futures Specifications
Trading Unit: 1 contract = 25,000 pounds
Prices Quoted: U.S. cents per pound
Trading Symbol: HG
Exchange: COMEX
Trading Months: Every month for 23 months out

Platinum Futures

Platinum has the distinction of being both an industrial metal and a precious metal. On the industrial side of things, platinum is used heavily by the dental, chemical, and electronics industries. The greatest industrial use for platinum, however, is used by the auto industry. Because of its chemical qualities, platinum is used in catalytic converters to reduce emissions.

The demand for platinum in catalytic converters has increased in the last several years due to the stricter regulations on fuel emissions. European countries use platinum extensively because it is a key component in diesel-fueled cars. Even in China, where emission regulations are not as strict, the government is looking at curbing pollution by initiating and enforcing stronger fuel emission policies. As more cars come on the road due to increased wealth and population growth, I expect platinum demand to increase in the industrial sector.

While the demand in the industrial sector is strong, the greatest demand for platinum comes from the precious metals industry, where more than half of platinum consumption comes in the form of jewelry. Once again, jewelry demand also increases as people have more discretionary income to spend. This is the case not just in industrializing nations but in developed nations as well.

If you have ever shopped for jewelry, you would have noticed that the price of platinum jewelry is double the price of gold jewelry. This is no coincidence. When it comes to deposits, platinum is 30 times rarer than gold, and deposits are found mostly in South Africa and Russia. Yet even though platinum is more expensive than gold, global demand for platinum has increased by over 35 percent over the last decade.

When it comes to supply, the global supply of platinum has failed to meet demand for seven straight years. I expect this trend will continue, especially since platinum is one of the rarest metals. If you are looking at purchasing platinum futures, you can trade the contracts on the COMEX in New York.

Platinum Futures Specifications
Trading Unit: 50 troy ounces
Prices Quoted: U.S. dollars and cents per troy ounce
Trading Symbol: PL

Exchange: COMEX

Trading Months: Trading occurs over a 15-month interval. It starts
with the first month and the following consecutive months. After
that, contracts trade on a quarterly basis in the following months:
January, April, July, and October

Palladium Futures

Palladium futures also trade on the COMEX but are three times cheaper
than the price of platinum futures. The price differential is significant,
especially since palladium has similar industrial uses as platinum. In other
words, the qualities of both metals allow for them to function in a similar
manner. For example, several years ago, the autocatalytic converter in
my wife's car needed to be replaced. The mechanic gave me a choice:
We could have an autocatalytic converter made of platinum or palladium. Both provided the same function, but one was cheaper than the
other.

Because palladium is less than half the cost of platinum, the demand
for palladium jewelry has also increased steadily over the last several years.
Most of this jewelry demand is coming from China, which accounts for
more than two-thirds of the global palladium jewelry demand. Palladium
is also used with gold to blend and form the increasingly popular white
gold.

When it comes to the long-term outlook for palladium, I believe
that it is one of the best value plays of this commodity bull market.
Whereas the other metals have soared during the first stage of this
commodity boom, palladium has lagged behind. In fact, not only has it
lagged behind, but it is significantly lower from its highs at the start of
this bull market.

Take a look at Figures 5.4 and 5.5. The first thing that you will likely
notice is the price discrepancy between both metals. At one time palladium was trading at over $1,000/ounce and was much more expensive
than platinum. Over the last decade, however, the trend has obviously
changed. While there are some differences between the two metals (e.g.,
palladium cannot be used in diesel autocatalytic converters), the general
industrial function is the same. I expect the gap between the two metals
to tighten considerably over the next several years. In fact, in terms of

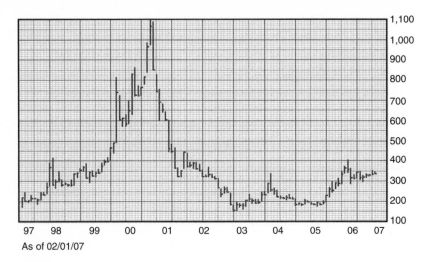

As of 02/01/07

Figure 5.4 Palladium (Monthly)
SOURCE: Barchart.com

percentage gains, palladium futures have increased more than platinum futures since palladium hit a low in the fall of 2005.

Palladium Futures Specifications
Trading Unit: 100 troy ounces
Prices Quoted: U.S. dollars and cents per troy ounce

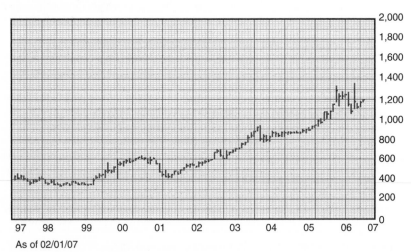

As of 02/01/07

Figure 5.5 Platinum (Monthly)
SOURCE: Barchart.com

Trading Symbol: PA
Exchange: COMEX
Trading Months: Trading occurs over a 15-month interval. It starts
with the first month and the following consecutive months. After
that, contracts trade on a quarterly basis in the following months:
March, June, September, and December

Gold Futures

Gold is a unique metal because not only does it have industrial and
precious metal qualities, but it is also used as a monetary commodity.
From gold coins to gold bullion, gold has been used as a form of money
since biblical times. In Chapter 11 I talk about gold as a monetary
commodity and the various ways that you can profit from this bull
market.

In regard to the gold futures market in the United States, gold trades
both on the COMEX and on the CBOT.

Gold Futures Specifications
Trading Unit: 100 troy ounces
Prices Quoted: U.S. dollars and cents per troy ounce
Trading Symbol: GC
Exchange: COMEX and CBOT
Trading Months: The contracts can go out 60 months. The first
and next calendar months are tradable. After the first two calendar
months, February, April, August, and October (falling within a
23-month period) and June and December (falling within a 60-
month period beginning with the current month).

Silver Futures

Mexico, Peru, and Australia are some of the top producers of silver in the
world. After silver is mined, it is typically used for jewelry, photography,
silverware, and in a diverse range of electronic products.

This is one key difference between gold and silver. Gold is used more
as a monetary commodity and for jewelry; silver is also heavily used in
industrial applications. Because of its industrial use, there is actually less

supply of silver aboveground today than there was 20 years ago. In other words, a lot of silver has been lost due to its use in the industrial sector. Not surprisingly, silver has been in a supply deficit for the last several decades.

Silver Futures Specifications
Trading Unit: 5,000 troy ounces
Prices Quoted: U.S. dollars and cents per troy ounce
Trading Symbol: SI
Exchange: COMEX
Trading Months: Contracts can go out 60 months. The first month and next two calendar months are tradable. After the first two calendar months, January, March, May, and September (falling within a 23-month period) and any July and December (falling within a 60-month period) beginning with the current month.

How You Can Participate in the Futures Market

There are several ways that you can participate in the futures market. For instance, you can trade your own account online or through a broker, you can participate in a managed futures fund, or you can give limited power of attorney to a commodity trading advisor, who will trade your individual account on your behalf. Deciding which path to take, once again, depends on your investment objective, risk profile, and preference.

If you are interested in trading your own account, I recommend that you find a commodity broker who can assist you with the various nuances associated with futures trading. For a slightly more expensive commission, you will get some guidance along the way. If you do not know of a good commodity broker, I recommend that you call several brokers and get a feel for their personality, commission charges, and general services. You can find a list of commodity brokers on various Web sites.

Once you find a broker, the account opening procedure should not be too difficult. Some firms allow you to open accounts online; others require you to fill out traditional new account forms. These new account forms are somewhat similar to typical stock brokerage account forms, in that they ask about personal information and investment objectives. When it comes to opening up a commodity brokerage account, there is no minimum opening requirement. However, I would be leery about opening up an account with only a few thousand dollars. That amount will only allow you to participate in one or two markets; and if the account pulls back, you will have to either liquidate your position or send in more money.

I also recommend that you look into some type of third-party assistance. I talk more about this in Chapter 12, but third-party assistance can be anything from financial newsletters that have specific recommendations on the futures market, to good, reputable brokers or even commodity trading systems that can assist you in trading the futures markets from a more technical perspective.

Conclusion

This chapter has provided a great deal of information. My goal was to introduce you not only to the diversity of the futures markets, but also to the different factors that can positively or negatively impact each market. In addition, I wanted to provide you with some actual examples of the futures market at work. In other words, although you might not be interested in live cattle futures, now you know why a rancher would want to hedge or why a butcher would want to lock in a certain price.

Beyond the markets that I listed, there are many more markets that you can use to profit from this long-term commodity boom. If you can think of a commodity that will be in high demand due to the fundamental factors discussed in Chapter 1, there is a good likelihood that it has a futures equivalent.

Many of the central themes (and supply and demand factors) discussed in Chapter 1 spill over to a wide variety of commodity markets. Whether it's the increased consumption of meat products or the increased demand for fuel, China has a significant impact on a wide spectrum of commodities. The same can be said about the supply situation of most commodities, hard and soft. Indeed, if you can recognize the factors that are significant in each sector and each market, you will have a better idea of how to profit from these markets. And futures, as an investment vehicle, will provide you with this opportunity.

Chapter 6

Participating Through Stocks

I know from experience that nobody can give me a tip or series of tips that will make money for me than my own judgment.

—Jesse Livermore

From a logistical perspective, it is relatively easy to participate in this commodity boom by buying shares of companies that profit from rising commodity prices. Since most investors are already familiar with buying Google or Microsoft stock, transitioning into buying the stock of a mining company or an energy company should not be too difficult. In fact, if you already have an online brokerage account or a stockbroker, buying commodity stocks should take no more than a click of the mouse or a verbal order over the phone.

But selecting which stocks to buy will take a little bit more effort on your part. First, you have to decide which companies will appreciate during various stages of this bull market. For instance, if you are bullish on energy, you will likely look at buying energy related companies. But which companies do you buy? Do you buy an oil company? Or do you buy a natural gas company? What about a company that produces both oil and natural gas? And let's not forget ethanol, coal, uranium, and other energy-related companies. You get the picture.

Once you determine which types of companies you want to buy, you then have to decide which specific company to purchase. Do you buy a large-cap stock or a small-cap stock? Do you put more value on a company that is established or on one that is aggressively growing? And what about the management of the company? Does it even matter that a company has a more experienced management team? In general, when you look at buying a commodity stock, you have to consider all the nuances associated with owning shares of any publicly traded company.

Not surprisingly, these factors also can change from day to day. On any given day, the company that you have been following can be purchased by another company. Perhaps a top executive of a company that you have in your portfolio decides to leave. Another scenario might be that an exploratory company receives negative results from one of its most costly ventures. Indeed, even when you buy shares of a company that you feel will profit from this commodity boom, certain situations can transpire that alter the company's longer-term prospects.

For this reason, instead of listing stocks that I believe will perform during the next stage of this bull market, I focus more on the different types of companies that make up the commodity stock complex and outline several questions that can help you decide which companies might be most appropriate for your portfolio. By understanding how these commodity companies function, you will be able to better adapt to changing markets.

A Closer Look at the Commodity Stock Complex

One of the first things that you will notice when you look at the commodity stock complex is that there are many more energy and mining companies than there are other commodity-related stocks. This is no coincidence. The different size of these markets is due partly to how the commodity is produced and the costs associated with producing it.

In the energy and metals sectors, there is a plethora of costs associated with bringing the usable commodity to the market. Exploring for the deposit is a costly and risky venture, then there's the cost of extracting the deposit and the cost to bring the usable commodity to the market. Moreover, there are many technological and upkeep costs associated with those industries. Consequently, it normally takes a lot of money to produce and profit from upward moves in the energy and metals markets. As you can imagine, most of the companies that have the type of cash to participate in these markets are large private corporations or publicly traded companies.

In contrast, most of the producers of food commodities are individuals or small privately held companies. Since the costs associated with producing these commodities are not as steep, a corn farmer from Iowa, a cattle rancher from Texas, and an orange grower from Florida can easily produce their respective commodity on their individual plot of land. Unfortunately, while the lower cost of production allows individuals to participate in the production of food commodities, it ultimately serves as a disadvantage to investors who want to use the stock market to profit from the agricultural commodity boom.

Indeed, this is one of the disadvantages to using only the stock market to participate in this long-term bull market in commodities. As I have pointed out, there will be various stages of this bull market. Sometimes energy and metals will lead the way, and other times agricultural commodities will appreciate the most. Not having the ability to profit from moves up in the grains, meats, and softs sectors can be a disadvantage to investors who are looking to profit from all aspects of this commodity bull market.

As an example, in January 2006, I wrote a market commentary stating that I believed that corn would stage a vicious rally. I received several e-mails from readers who wanted to know which corn-producing companies I would recommend. Regrettably, I couldn't recommend any. If people wanted to profit from rising corn prices, they had to do so by participating in the corn futures market.

Some companies do profit from rising agricultural prices. However, these companies are few and far between. In addition, most profit only by providing products and services for the agricultural industry or by selling a refined version of the commodity. For example, if there is an increased demand for agricultural commodities, there will be an increased demand for companies that provide fertilizer, farm equipment, transportation services, and processing and storage facilities. Consequently, it only makes sense that companies that provide those services will appreciate from the increase in demand in agricultural commodities.

While it is often difficult to find many companies that profit from higher agricultural prices, it is relatively easy to find companies that directly and indirectly profit from the energy and metals boom. If you look back at the first stage of this bull market, you can find scores of energy and mining stocks that profited from increased demand for energy and metals. You can distinguish among the different companies that make up the energy and mining sectors not only by their underlying commodity, but also by the scope and nature of their business.

Companies that Produce . . .

In both the energy and mining sectors, you will find companies that profit from producing and selling some version of the physical commodities. These types of companies own the actual gold mine, copper mine, or oil well. If you are looking at finding the purest play in the commodity stock complex, buying shares in a commodity producer is probably your best option. This is because the revenue of the company is dependent on the price of the physical commodity that it sells.

Focusing on the actual commodity that the company produces is another way that you can differentiate among the different commodity producers. You can further distinguish companies that produce the same commodities by focusing on their reserves. For example, if you are looking at purchasing a gold mining stock, you may come across a wide array of different companies. Some might hold rights to a single mine in Canada, others might have a couple of small mines, and others might have several large mines across multiple countries. As you can imagine, buying shares in a large and established gold mining company is a lot different from buying shares in a smaller company. Not only does a large company have proven and diversified reserves, but it also has the capital to continually look for new projects and grow its profitability. In short, even though both are gold mining stocks, they are different types of companies that are subject to different types of problems and different types of returns.

Further complicating the organizational structure of commodity producers is the fact that several companies produce a number of different commodities. Thus, when you buy shares in a gold mining company, you might also be buying shares in a company that produces copper and a couple of other industrial metals. In the case of some commodity conglomerates, buying shares in the company will offer exposure across a number of commodity sectors. For instance, BHP Billiton is a commodity conglomerate made up of seven different divisions. Not only does the company produce a variety of metals, but it is also a producer of oil and gas.

...and Companies that Provide Products and Services

Just as there are some companies that profit from providing products and services to the agricultural industry, there are also companies that profit by providing products and services to the energy and mining industries. The difference, however, is that there are a lot more of these companies around. Of course, this makes sense. As I stated earlier, bringing the finished commodity to the market is significantly more cost intensive in the energy and metals sectors than it is in the other commodity sectors. Therefore, many of these companies have been able to profit from moves in the energy and metals markets.

As an example, consider these four companies that fall under the oil category. While they all profit from higher oil prices, they have different business models.

Transocean (RIG): RIG provides oil companies with offshore exploratory equipment and services. In essence, the company aids oil and gas companies in exploration for new deposits. With increased demand and higher oil prices, oil-producing companies will spend more money looking for new deposits.

Ultra Petroleum (UPL): UPL is an oil and gas exploration and production company. Its primary properties are located in the Green River Basin (Wyoming) and Bohai Bay (China). The company profits from the higher energy prices by selling and producing the physical commodity. Since 2001, production has increased by an annual compound rate of 67 percent.

Baker Hughes International (BHI): BHI provides oil companies with a diverse offering of products and services. The company operates in over 90 countries and provides everything from drill bits to production management services. BHI falls under the oil services classification.

Knightsbridge Tankers Limited (VLCCF): VLCCF is a shipping company that is primarily responsible for transporting crude oil. With global oil demand increasing yearly, the demand for the limited number of oil tankers has also increased. As a result, VLCCF, Frontline Tech, and other oil shipping companies have been able to command top dollar to transport the oil. VLCCF has historically paid a double-digit yearly dividend yield and has still managed to appreciate along with higher oil prices.

While all of these companies appreciated during the first stage, they appreciated in varying degrees and for various reasons. Ultra Petroleum's stock price moved higher because it was able to produce and sell more crude oil. Baker Hughes's appreciation was a result of the increased need for products and services by the larger oil companies. Transocean appreciated because part of the profits from the larger oil companies was poured into exploration projects, and Knightsbridge moved higher because there was a continued energy demand in both developed and developing economies and there was a need for fuel transportation.

Commodity Stocks Reaffirming a Bull Market

I want to point out a couple of other things about the four companies I just introduced. First, the simultaneous appreciation of a diverse group of energy-related companies is a reaffirmation of the current bull market in energy. If there was no increased demand for oil, there would be no need for Ultra Petroleum and other oil-producing companies to spend money on the products and services of companies like Transocean and Baker Hughes. Furthermore, if there was no viable increase in the use of crude oil by consumers in both developed and developing economies, there would be no increased demand for oil tankers. Of course, over the first stage of this commodity bull market, energy companies posted record earnings. In 2006, for example, Baker Hughes reported a 29 percent increase in year-over-year net income. The sizable increase was attributed to increased revenue from its drilling and evaluation business.

Another point to take away is that during this bull market in commodities, not all of the companies that deal with the same commodity will appreciate in the same manner. A company that finds a large deposit of oil will undoubtedly appreciate more than the company that provided drilling services for that oil field. The companies also have different roles in different portfolios. For instance, if your portfolio was made up primarily of dividend-paying investments, you might not want to take a chance on a small speculative oil stock. Rather, you would probably look at allocating money toward a large oil company that had established reserves and even paid a dividend. Conversely, if you had a more aggressive portfolio, buying shares in a speculative oil stock might not be a bad idea. If the company finds a substantial oil deposit, its share price might appreciate several times over.

How to Choose the Right Commodity Stocks for Your Portfolio

For some reason, the general stock market investor has a fixation with the hot stock tip. You need only to turn on the financial television networks to see shows dedicated to recommending the next hot stock. During the Internet boom, countless friends told me about the next great company. Since my friends lived in Silicon Valley, they believed they had added insight into the technology and Internet world. On one occasion, they told me about an Internet company that would revolutionize the business world as we know it. Not only would the demand for the product increase substantially over the next several years, but the current stock price was unbelievably cheap. The stock, they argued, would triple if not quadruple in value over a short period of time. I just had to get in. Of course, when I took a closer look at the company, it was not even cash flow positive. Nonetheless, these friends believed that paying $100 a share for a company that was in the red was not only a good bargain but a hot stock tip.

Perhaps you had a similar situation where you bought a stock based on the recommendation of a friend, a neighbor, or even a financial expert. And even though you might cringe at those memories, you still desire to invest in a company that will be the best performer. When it comes to commodity stocks, you want to know which stocks will be sure things. I will even venture to guess that there are some people who purchased this book to find out about which hot commodity stock they should purchase. Unfortunately, I don't have any hot commodity stock tips for you. However, I can provide you with this long-term stock tip: When you buy shares of a commodity stock, you should consider the company's long-term prospects.

From my experience, it seems that many people buy shares in a company without giving much thought to the fact that they are becoming part owners in it. In any other circumstance, I would imagine that buying part of a company would result in a lot of due diligence and a more long-term outlook. For example, if you decided to buy a local restaurant, you would look not only at its short-term profitability but at its long-term prospects. You might focus on the demographics, demand for the product, and general market trends. You would do all of this because this is not just a short-term investment; you are investing your money and want to make sure that it is a successful venture.

You should have the same attitude when you invest in a commodity stock. Don't fall for the next hot tip, just because the company happens to be outperforming the market. Although there is a chance that you will make some short-term money, there is also a great chance that you will have purchased a momentum play that lacks the infrastructure, the deposits, or the management to make it a viable long-term investment. So when you are considering buying the next hot commodity stock, be sure to ask yourself this question: Do you want to be a part owner of this company . . . or are there better options?

There are some other questions that you can ask that can help you determine which commodity stock to buy.

Is the Company on the Right Side of the Commodity Trend?

Just as different commodity futures markets profit from different stages of the commodity boom, different commodity stocks will appreciate during different times of this commodity bull market. Energy stocks will likely appreciate as the energy sector appreciates; mining stocks will move as the overall metals sector moves; and agricultural-related stocks will head higher as specific markets in the grains sector head higher. As a result, it is important to buy shares in companies that are on the right side of the commodity trend.

While this question seems obvious, it is also the most crucial. Your primary goal is to invest in a company that is on the right side of the commodity trend. In other words, pay attention to the prevailing market conditions of its underlying commodity. If the price of a commodity seems to be in the early stages of a downward decline, buying shares in a company that will profit from rising commodity prices might not be the best decision. Conversely, if you believe that a certain commodity is undervalued and will likely appreciate, then buying shares in a company that produces that commodity makes sense. This is yet another reason that it is in your best interest to understand the commodity futures market.

Of course, to determine the general direction of the commodity trend, you must understand the fundamentals of the specific commodity markets. While the long-term fundamentals for a specific commodity might point to higher prices, there will undoubtedly be times when commodity prices get ahead of themselves and are due for an intermediate correction. If you are more of a buy-and-hold type investor, you might view intermediate-term movements as irrelevant over the long term. However, if you are not a buy-and-hold investor, you must be cognizant of intermediate market trends that occur.

Take, for example, the trends we have seen in the oil market over the last five years. Even though oil prices have seemingly hit new highs during this first stage of the bull market, there have been intermediate trends that have resulted in a sizable depreciation in the price of oil. The price of oil dropped substantially in both 2002 and 2006. During these times of depreciation, oil companies happened to be on the wrong side of the intermediate commodity trend; consequently, many oil-related companies experienced sizable declines in their stock price.

Does the Company Fit with Your Overall Portfolio Goals?

Once again, I want to point out that not all portfolios are alike. Thus, the types of companies that make up the various portfolios will also differ. When deciding which natural resource company to buy, you have to consider whether it fits with your overall portfolio goals. Investors often get carried away with buying shares of companies that do not necessarily fit with their overall objectives. For instance, if your objective is to have a portfolio that is made up primarily of large-cap, dividend-paying investments, it might not make sense to buy shares of a mining company that is speculating on finding gold. Smaller mining companies typically pay no dividends and are substantially more volatile than larger and more established companies. Conversely, if your portfolio is more aggressive in nature, you might want to consider investing in a smaller speculative gold mining company. While the risk is greater, the return can also be greater.

The idea here is that you can participate in this commodity bull market by buying a variety of commodity stocks. When looking at the ones to select for your portfolio, make sure you pick those that fit your goals. Don't waste your time following companies that you should have no business owning. Rather, follow the type of companies that will complement your other investments and meet your objectives.

Additionally, when looking at the various commodity companies, make sure that you don't oversaturate your portfolio with companies of similar types. Don't have a portfolio composed only of energy and mining stocks. While this portfolio might prove profitable when those sectors increase, you will also experience greater declines when those sectors correct.

Does the Company Have Strong Fundamentals?

Once you decide which types of commodity stocks you should purchase for your portfolio, you should start looking at the company's fundamentals. Keep in mind that just because a company produces a commodity does not mean that you should blindly purchase stock in that company. Several other factors determine the profitability of a company. Taking time to review the company's fundamentals is important if you are going to select a strong company for your portfolio. This reiterates my earlier point about buying a company that you would like to own.

While looking at the company's fundamentals might seem like a job for a full-time analyst, it really is not as difficult as it seems. Furthermore, the little extra effort might pay dividends down the line. An easy way to check fundamentals is by accessing the company's quarterly or annual reports. Most companies have these reports right on their Web sites. Among other things, these reports outline the costs, revenue stream, and profitability of the company. Typically, for most companies, you will want to look for ones that have an increasing revenue stream and a growing level of profitability.

> **TIP**
>
> *Know your limitations.* If you do not have the time or desire to actively trade or research the commodity markets, find a manager, broker, or managed fund that will do this on your behalf.

Another factor that you want to look at is the historical performance of the company. How has it performed during the first stage of this bull market? If the share price has increased, how has it performed relative to similar companies? If a company has continually outperformed its competitors, try to find out why. Is it more efficient? Does it have better reserves? Generally speaking, there is a reason why a company consistently outperforms its peers.

If you would rather not spend time reading through company fundamentals, a number of third-party sources can help you. In Chapter 12, I discuss some advisory newsletters and other services that can help you with your stock selection.

What Are the Long-Term Prospects of the Company?

Since we are in a long-term bull market in commodities, you will also want to consider the long-term prospects of the company that you are buying. This means a couple of things. First, once again you have to look at the long-term commodity trends. Second, you must look at the company's long-term growth prospects. For commodity producers, this means focusing on the company's current levels of reserves. Since hard commodities are finite in nature, it is only a matter of time until an oil well comes up dry or a copper mine in Chile shuts down. Consequently, it is important to invest in companies that have enough reserves to profit continually from this commodity boom.

Additionally, it is also important to know whether commodity producers are spending money on exploration projects for new deposits. Not only does this reaffirm the company's belief that there will be a long-term demand for its raw materials, but it will also aid in building up the company's reserves for the future.

In the case of commodity companies that are not commodity producers, it is still important to look at their long-term growth prospects. How are they adapting to changing market trends? As an example, Archer Daniels Midland (ADM), a company that provides products and services to the agricultural industry, responded to the growing ethanol demand by spending hundreds of millions of dollars on expanding and building new ethanol facilities. In light of the growing demand for a cheaper and more environmentally friendly fuel alternative, ADM was willing to spend money in the short term to profit over the long term.

Does the Management Hold on to the Same Bull Market Goals?

This might seem like another simple question, but you would be surprised by how many companies fail to fully profit from this bull market because of their outlook. Even though the management of most commodity companies will have a bullish outlook, some companies fail to put their words into action. If you scan the commodity stock universe, you will find some companies that are aggressively capitalizing from this bull market by expanding their business and taking other actions. For example, some companies might acquire rivals for a substantial premium; others might increase the amount of money they are allocating to exploratory projects; still others might expand their current facilities and manufacturing plants in anticipation of greater demand.

On the flip side, there are also companies that fail to expand their business. These companies will take a more status quo approach and choose to bypass any new and costly ventures. Furthermore, some companies even decide to hedge their physical commodities. By doing so, they limit their upside move because they must pay for the additional hedging costs. Not surprisingly, their hedging tactics ultimately affect their stock price.

Thus, it makes sense to purchase companies that not only express a bullish outlook but also put their outlook it into action.

Why No Stock Picks?

If you are interested in actual stock picks, various books, several dozen newsletters, and a couple of financial news shows can offer you both good and bad advice on which commodity stocks to purchase. My goal in writing this chapter was not to provide you with a list of companies that you could invest in; rather, my goal was to provide you with a guide for selecting the type of companies that might be appropriate for your portfolio. Once you understand the different types of companies that directly and indirectly profit from this commodity bull market, you can more easily figure out which ones will profit from rising commodity prices.

The second thing to realize is that companies are always changing. It is important to understand the underlying reasons why a company is profitable, rather than investing in a company simply because a friend recommended it or because it has been mentioned several times on the local television channel. As an example, I could have easily listed several companies that I believe will profit from this commodity demand. However, there is a good possibility that by the time you read this book, many of the factors that I like about the company might have changed.

Conclusion

Buying into this commodity bull market through commodity stocks takes some additional due diligence to find out which companies are better positioned to profit from rising raw material costs. Nonetheless, if you focus on some key factors, you should be able to find the type of company that will profit from higher commodity prices today and in the future.

Indeed, you should purchase stock in commodity companies with a long-term outlook. While momentum plays might make money in the short term, companies that have a viable business model and infrastructure in place will more effectively profit from the continued supply and demand imbalance in the commodity marketplace.

Chapter 7

Participating Through Mutual Funds

The only source of knowledge is experience.

—Albert Einstein

Since the start of this bull market, there has clearly been an increase in the number of mutual funds that fall under the natural resource and commodity sectors. If you look at the different commodity mutual funds today, you will notice that most do not have a track record that goes beyond five years. The emergence of additional commodity mutual funds has occurred as many fund companies have positioned themselves to participate in a sector that has outperformed other sectors over the last several years. This growth has provided additional options for investors who want to use commodity mutual funds as their primary investment vehicle for participating in this long-term commodity boom.

In this chapter I look at the various types of commodity mutual funds as well as the pros and cons of investing in mutual funds and what factors you should look for when selecting mutual funds.

Scanning the Mutual Fund World

In a way, commodity mutual funds epitomize the various ways that you can profit from this long-term commodity boom. You can invest in mutual funds that invest in stocks, or you can invest in mutual funds that invest in futures. You can also invest in mutual funds that cater toward a specific sector, or you can invest in mutual funds that cover a variety of sectors. Indeed, investing in a commodity mutual fund can mean a number of different things. All told, several hundred different types of mutual funds fall under several categories. While these mutual funds are all built to profit from rising commodity prices, they differ in their makeup and commodity representation.

One of the better and simpler ways of scanning the various commodity mutual funds is by accessing financial Web sites that provide a basic exposure to the commodity mutual fund world. Generally speaking, these sites are all pretty much the same. If you are not accustomed to viewing financial Web sites, here is a sample of sites that offer information and screening abilities on mutual funds:

www.bloomberg.com
www.marketwatch.com
http://finance.yahoo.com
http://money.cnn.com

By visiting these sites, you accomplish several things. First, you can view the performance of the commodity mutual funds over several time frames. This can provide insight on which funds have the best cumulative performance over a longer period of time and can also provide insight on the best-performing funds over a shorter, more recent period. Most of these sites will even rank the different funds over multiple time frames.

Additionally, these sites contain information on the manager, a list of their major holdings, their fees, and a number of other snapshots that can give you a clearer, albeit cursory, overview. If you are interested in no-load funds, you can focus strictly on the funds that do not charge a load. Similarly, if you are interested in a specific fund family, you can view the commodity funds that are a part of that fund family. In other words, you can use these sites to narrow down which mutual funds will require further research on your part.

Once you look at the various mutual funds, you will notice that a handful of mutual funds fall under the commodity index category, while the majority fall under the natural resource category. Structurally, they are all pretty much the same; you are buying into an investment portfolio that is being managed by an investment company. However, there are some distinct differences between the commodity index funds and natural resource funds. I focus on this later in the chapter.

Commodity Index Funds

Commodity index funds are mutual funds that track a specific futures index. These funds typically invest in a mixture of commodity-linked derivative instruments (i.e., futures contracts, futures options, and swaps) and fixed income securities. The difference between the index funds breaks down to the percentage they allocate toward following the index, their money management strategies (which type of fixed income securities they purchase), expenses, and, of course, which index the fund tracks.

For instance, take a look at the different commodity indexes and their respective mutual funds. While you will notice certain similarities among the different indexes, they differ in respect to weighting and the inclusion of some different commodities.

Dow Jones-AIG Commodity Index

The Dow Jones-AIG Commodity Index (DJ-AIGCI) is composed of futures contracts on 19 different commodities that are spread out across the different futures sectors. Besides aluminum, nickel, and zinc (which trade on the London Metals Exchange), the commodities that make up the DJ-AIGCI trade on U.S. commodity exchanges.

The composition and weightings of the index are determined by an oversight committee that meets on a yearly basis. The committee looks at a number of different factors to determine which commodities make up the index and the percentage of their allocation. When it comes to data, the committee mostly focuses on liquidity data. In other words, the commodities that are the most liquid and actively traded will have the highest percentage allocation. The logic here is that these are the most consumed commodities and represent the world's demand for them. In addition to the liquidity data, the DJ-AIGCI also focuses on dollar-adjusted production data.

In order to ensure a diversified index, the DJ-AIGCI also stipulates that no specific sector will make up greater than one-third of the index. Similarly, no specific commodity will make up more than 15 percent and less than 2 percent of the index. You can see this clearly in Table 7.1, which shows the percentage weightings that make up the index (dated January 2007).

The Pacific Investment Management Company (PIMCO) Commodity Real Return Fund and the Credit Suisse Commodity Return Strategy Fund are two open-ended funds that are set up to track the

Table 7.1   Dow Jones-AIG Commodity Index

Commodity	Percentage Weighting (%)
Natural Gas	12.546191
Crude Oil	12.723561
Unleaded Gas (RBOB)	3.940958
Heating Oil	3.789289
Live Cattle	6.141286
Lean Hogs	3.013524
Wheat	4.715495
Corn	5.627129
Soybeans	7.747790
Soybean Oil	2.845646
Aluminum	6.803820
Copper	6.187758
Zinc	2.798069
Nickel	2.715318
Gold	6.825901
Silver	2.288179
Sugar	3.122271
Cotton	3.146094
Coffee	3.021718

performance of the Dow Jones-AIGCI. In regard to cash management, PIMCO Commodity Real Return is an example of how the index funds differ in their cash management strategies. Rather than investing in a variety of regular treasuries, the PIMCO Commodity Real Return Fund invests in Treasury Inflated Protected Securities (TIPS). TIPS differ from other treasuries in that their yield is less, but the principal and interest is increased with rising inflation. Therefore, in a rising inflation environment, you will most likely see the actual fund outperform the index.

Goldman Sachs Commodity Index

The Goldman Sachs Commodity Index (GSCI) is a weighted index comprised of 24 commodity futures contracts that are spread across the various market sectors. The composition is determined by a policy committee that meets on an annual basis. See Table 7.2 for the composition of the GSCI as of January 2007.

In contrast to the DJ-AIGCI, the GSCI does not have a cap on the weightings for each commodity sector, nor does it take into account liquidity data. Instead, the actual percentage of each commodity is determined by the average of the amount of production of the commodity over the last five years. The net result is that the GSCI has a much greater weighting in the energy sector.

The Black Rock Real Investment Fund and Rydex Fund are two mutual funds that track the performance of the GSCI.

Other Index Funds

Besides the mutual funds that track the GSCI and the DJ-AIGCI, a handful of other mutual funds track other indexes. Brookshire Raw Materials has a number of funds that track a variety of indexes. Their flagship index is the Brookshire International Raw Materials Index (BIRMI), shown in Table 7.3.

One of the interesting aspects of Brookshire Raw Materials is that the company also has a number of funds that track more focused commodity indexes. Specifically, the company has a metals, energy, and agricultural index. The indices are constructed by taking the commodities that are part of the BIRMI and weighing them based

Table 7.2   Goldman Sachs Commodity Index (GSCI)

Commodity	Percentage Weighting (%)
Crude Oil	30.50
Brent Crude Oil	14.81
Unleaded Gas (RBOB)	2.32
Heating Oil	8.35
Gas Oil	4.51
Natural Gas	8.60
Aluminum	3.57
Copper	4.18
Lead	0.44
Nickel	1.51
Zinc	1.59
Gold	2.09
Silver	0.31
Wheat	3.24
Red Wheat	1.15
Corn	3.52
Soybeans	1.60
Cotton	0.87
Sugar	1.36
Coffee	0.78
Cocoa	0.19
Live Cattle	2.45
Feeder Cattle	0.59
Lean Hogs	1.46

on their percent allocation in the flagship index. For instance, the Brookshire Raw Materials Index Metals (BRMME) is comprised of nine metal commodities (see Table 7.4).

Index funds that are focused on specific sectors offer the advantage of providing you with opportunities from various stages of this commodity bull market. If you are bullish on agriculture and intermediately bearish on energy, the agricultural-specific fund will provide you with a better opportunity to implement your strategy. You cannot do this with the more diversified index funds.

Another interesting aspect of Brookshire Raw Materials is that it allows you to keep your cash investments in a variety of currencies. This

Table 7.3 Brookshire International Raw Materials Index (BIRMI)

Agriculture		Metals	
Grains		Industrial Metals	
Barley	0.50%	Aluminum	3.50%
Corn	4.00%	Copper	5.00%
Wheat	6.00%	Lead	3.00%
Rough Rice	1.50%	Nickel	3.00%
Soybeans	3.50%	Tin	2.50%
Softs		Zinc	2.50%
Coffee	1.50%	Precious Metals	
Sugar	1.50%	Gold	3.00%
Cotton	2.00%	Platinum	3.00%
Livestock		Silver	3.00%
Lean Hogs	2.00%	Metals Total	28.50%
Live Cattle	2.00%	Energy	
Paper and Forests		Brent Crude	6.50%
Lumber	1.50%	Crude	23.00%
Rubber	1.00%	Heating Oil	5.00%
Agriculture Total	27.00%	Natural Gas	5.00%
		RBOB	5.00%
		Energy Total	44.50%
		Total	100.00%

can be an added benefit for individuals who might be concerned with the depreciation of the U.S. dollar. Instead of keeping the money in U.S. dollars, you can have the money held in Canadian dollars, U.K. pounds sterling, euros, or Japanese yen.

Table 7.4 Brookshire Raw Materials Index Metals (BRMME)

Industrial Metals		Precious Metals	
Copper	17.50%	Gold	10.50%
Aluminum	12.00%	Silver	10.50%
Lead	10.50%	Platinum	10.50%
Nickel	10.50%	Subtotal	31.50%
Tin	9.00%		
Zinc	9.00%		
Subtotal	68.50%	Total	100.00%

Natural Resource Funds

Natural resource funds also provide mutual fund investors with an opportunity to profit from this commodity bull market. As I stated earlier, a natural resource fund is simply a mutual fund made up of natural resource companies. In reality, this is no different from any other traditional mutual fund. You are buying into a fund that is managed by a fund manager who selects which companies to purchase (as long as they fall under the natural resource category) and the percentage allocated toward each company. Since so many different types of companies profit from the commodity markets, a larger number of mutual funds fall under this category.

Within the natural resource funds category, however, mutual funds generally fall within one of three subcategories:

1. *Diversified natural resource funds.* These mutual funds are made up of a diverse group of commodity companies. Their portfolios are composed of any companies that fall under the natural resource category. Do not be surprised, however, to find that a number of these diversified natural resource funds still are heavily focused on the energy and metal sectors. Nonetheless, these mutual funds give you some type of exposure in companies that participate in other commodities, such as forestry products and agricultural companies.
2. *Energy-focused funds.* These funds invest strictly in companies that profit from rising energy prices. If you want to participate strictly in the energy bull market, you want to look at these types of mutual funds.
3. *Precious metals/metals funds.* These funds are comprised of companies that fall under the precious or industrial metals sectors. Some financial sites categorize these mutual funds in their own individual category. In other words, you will see a natural resource funds sector and a precious metals sector.

What's the Difference?

Even though they both fall under the category of mutual funds, there are several notable differences between a natural resource fund and a commodity index fund. The first difference has to do with how the funds are managed. With an index fund, the fund passively tracks a predetermined index. Beyond the decision of which treasuries to purchase, the fund typically replicates the movement of the actual index. Since the index itself rarely changes, you pretty much know what you are getting yourself into. With a natural resource fund, however, the fund manager has a more active role; he or she decides which companies should be part of the portfolio and their weightings. Obviously, this can change on a daily basis. In addition, you have the other risk factors that are associated with stocks (see Chapter 6). In any case, it is much more important to pay attention to the manager and past performance of a natural resource fund than it is to an index fund.

The second notable difference between the two types of funds has to do with the fact that one is composed of futures while the other is composed of stocks. If you recall the discussion of futures as a diversifying asset class, you will realize that this is a very distinct difference. Certain advantages come with participating in the futures market that you simply will not find by buying stocks or a mutual fund made up of stocks.

Moreover, certain advantages also come with the purchase of commodity index funds. In a March 2006 study commissioned by PIMCO, Ibbotson and Associates looked at the role of commodity index funds in the average portfolio, among other things. One of the factors that they looked at was Robert Greer's Commodity Futures Pricing Model. I don't want to get too specific in this discussion, but the general idea behind Greer's model is that additional factors, such as returns on treasury yield, insurance premium, rebalancing, and expectational variance, result in positive returns. In other words, because of these additional factors, commodity index returns are inherently positive.

Thus, when you compare the two types of commodity mutual funds, you can clearly see that there are obvious differences.

Pros and Cons of Commodity Mutual Funds

Depending on your portfolio structure and preferred style of investing, using commodity mutual funds to participate in this commodity bull market offers several advantages and disadvantages. Diversification, low minimum requirement, professional management, and fees are just a few factors that differentiate commodity mutual funds from other investments.

Diversification

There are several benefits when it comes to participating in the commodity bull market via commodity mutual funds. Whether it is a commodity index fund, a natural resource fund, or even a specific precious metals mutual fund, buying shares in a commodity mutual fund immediately diversifies your portfolio. In the case of the commodity index fund, your purchase exposes you to the different commodities that make up the index; if you decide to purchase shares in a natural resource fund, your exposure is spread across the different types of natural resource companies that are part of the portfolio; and even in the case of an energy or precious metals fund, your investment is diversified across several different types of energy or mining companies.

The aspect of diversification is beneficial in two ways. First, it lowers your overall risk by spreading your designated investment across a number of different commodities or companies. This is extremely important in an era where fraudulent accounting or other unforeseen circumstances can significantly alter a company's share price within a short period of time. Thus, by investing in a diversified fund, you don't have to worry about your money riding on the prospects of just one or two companies. The same can be said about not having all your money riding on just one commodity or one sector. When certain commodities decline, you can at least have several companies that will not be negatively affected.

The second beneficial aspect of this diversification is that you will gain exposure across a variety of different commodity markets and commodity companies that you typically would not purchase. Take, for example, the PIMCO Real Return Fund. Not only will your purchase expose you to the more common commodity markets, but you will also be able to profit from some obscure markets (lean hogs, live cattle, and soybean oil). In the case of natural resource funds, the fund manager might invest in some smaller mining companies that you would otherwise not own.

Yet there are also some negatives to buying a diversified mutual fund. When you purchase the mutual fund, you pretty much are stuck with every position in the portfolio. For instance, you might find yourself in a mutual fund that holds several companies that you would otherwise not purchase. Similarly, in an index fund, you might find yourself exposed to a commodity that you feel will likely depreciate in the next couple of years.

Low Minimum Requirements

While diversification in the commodity markets is great, you typically need to have a sizable amount of money to gain fairly diversified exposure. This is especially true if you want to buy a basket of commodity futures. The margin requirement for one commodity contract typically is more than the minimum of some commodity mutual funds. When it comes to commodity mutual funds, however, the minimum is extremely low due to the format of the fund. As a result, some commodity mutual funds allow you to buy units with a $500 minimum investment. For investors who have a limited amount of capital and who would like to participate in the commodity bull market in a diversified manner, commodity mutual funds can provide them with some good opportunities.

Of course, the low minimum requirement might be an irrelevant benefit for investors who have more sizable portfolios.

Professional Management

Another advantage of buying shares or units of a mutual fund is that you are buying into an investment that is managed by a professional money manager. Again, this can be irrelevant to more hands-on investors, but it can be extremely beneficial for those who do not want to watch their portfolio on a daily basis. Also, it can be advantageous to investors who do not want to spend the time researching when to buy or sell a certain natural resource company and how many shares of each company that they should purchase.

Managers of mutual funds typically have the education, the resources, the experience, and the full-time research staff to determine which companies to purchase. Moreover, they have the professional ability to determine how much to allocate toward each company and how much of their portfolio to keep in cash, and to cope with a number of other questions that arise from dealing in commodity stocks.

Nevertheless, professional management can also be a major disadvantage. Just because a person is a fund manager does not necessarily mean that he or she can navigate the fund successfully through this bull market. It is entirely possible to buy a commodity fund that is directed by a manager who does not have as bullish of a focus on the commodity markets. Thus, if this is the case, his stock selection might be more cautions and his returns less stellar than his peers or if you would have selected the stocks yourself.

Thus, it is possible to enter a commodity fund that is directed by a manager who does not have the same focus on the markets as you do.

Fees

It goes without saying that one has to pay for anything that is professionally managed and is structured to allow investors to participate in multiple investments for a minimum amount. The fees range from loads that you have to pay to enter the fund to a variety of expense fees that are generally attributed with running the fund. For many investors, it does not make sense to pay additional fees for a portfolio of stocks that they could buy for themselves. For others, the fees are well worth the benefits that come with being in a commodity mutual fund.

Choosing the Right Commodity Mutual Fund for Your Portfolio

There are a lot of different options when it comes to selecting which type of commodity mutual funds to have in your portfolio. Just as I do not list specific stock recommendations, it would be pointless for me to list specific commodity funds, especially for natural resource funds, whose portfolio is continuously changing. Nonetheless, I have no doubt that commodity mutual funds will be an option for many investors who prefer to have a managed and diversified exposure to the commodity markets.

Once again, deciding which commodity is right for your portfolio falls back to your specific portfolio goals. If you want to have a diversified exposure to commodities, then concentrating on energy-focused funds might not be the best idea. Rather than rehash what I have already discussed in previous chapters, I want to point out several things about selecting commodity mutual funds.

Select a Fund That Has an Established Track Record or Established Manager

You want to find a mutual fund that has either an established track record or an established manager. If the fund is an index fund, the track record of the mutual fund does not matter as much. You can just look at how the index has performed over the last several years. However, if you are buying a mutual fund that is actively managed, you want to at least examine how the manager has performed during the last several years.

Checking this is so important because it will give you insight into the manager's stock-picking abilities. You can also see what types of companies the manager likes. Does the manager purchase primarily big-name companies, or does he or she also allocate a portion of the portfolio to smaller and more value-oriented companies? If you find a new manager who has no experience, you are entering into the fund blindly. An experienced manager who has navigated effectively through this first stage of the commodity markets has a track record that can vouch for his or her aptitude.

Compare Similar Funds

When reviewing the different types of commodity funds, you want to compare apples to apples. For instance, comparing the PIMCO Commodity Real Return Fund with the Vanguard Energy Fund would not make sense. One fund invests in a diversified futures index, while the other invests in energy stocks. As a result, you cannot really tell which has performed better in various market environments.

You want to look for funds that have a similar focus and composition. For example, if you want to invest in an energy-focused fund, comparing the performance (over multiple time frames) and holdings will give you a clearer picture of which fund you might want to purchase. You will likely notice that some funds have consistently outperformed their peers over the last several years. This is a testament to the stock-picking abilities of the fund manager.

Review Their Holdings

Reviewing a mutual fund's holdings can give you a better idea of where you are putting your money. In a way, it is almost like looking under the hood of a car. You will be able to tell which companies the manager likes, the percentage that is allocated to the companies, and even the variety of the companies. For instance, if you are looking at investing a diversified natural resource fund, you will want to find a mutual fund that has a diversified portfolio of companies that goes beyond just metals and energy. While these positions can change, you can at least get an idea of the potential focus of the manager.

Read the Prospectus

Too many investors fail to read a fund's prospectus because they feel that they already know what they need to know. However, I highly recommend that you read the prospectus before you enter into a fund. A fund's prospectus give you detailed information on the fund's strategy as well as a detailed fee structure and other information that will help you make an informed decision.

Conclusion

Commodity mutual funds can provide you with the means to invest in the commodity markets from a more diversified and managed approach. The difference between commodity mutual funds and stocks or futures is that your commodity exposure is based on the selection of a manager or a pre-established index. While this might be an ideal scenario for some investors, it is not for investors who prefer a more hands-on and active approach to this commodity bull market.

Nonetheless, using commodity mutual funds as an investment vehicle will give you adequate exposure to this bull market. Evidence from previous years proves that some of the best-performing mutual funds have been those that have benefited from rising commodity or commodity stock prices.

Chapter 8

Participating Through Exchange-Traded Funds

He who waits upon fortune is never sure of dinner.

—Benjamin Franklin

Exchange-traded funds (ETFs) have been used by institutions for several decades, but only recently have investors been able to take advantage of this creative investment product. Over the last several years, Barclay's Global Investors, Vanguard, and a number of different investment companies have rolled out a variety of new ETFs. Initially these funds focused solely on tracking a basket of stocks, like the Standard & Poor's (S&P) 500. More recently, however, these companies have branched out to create ETFs that track several different commodity indices, commodity stocks, single commodities, and commodity currencies.

ETFs provide another way to participate in the long-term commodity boom in a more active and cost-effective manner. In this chapter I look at the differences between commodity ETFs and commodity index mutual funds, the advantages that ETFs can bring to your investment portfolio, and some of the different commodity ETFs that currently are available.

A Short Introduction to Exchange-Traded Funds

Even though ETFs are mentioned relatively frequently in the investment world, most people are still not clear on how these vehicles work or the advantages they can bring to a portfolio. Perhaps this has to do with the fact that there are so many differences among the various ETF products. For instance, not only are there hundreds of different ETFs, but they are also constructed differently; you can buy shares in an ETF that represents a holding in physical gold, or you can buy shares in an ETF that represents an interest in a fund that tracks a commodity futures index. Adding to this confusion is the fact that many ETFs are referred to by different names. Barclay's Global Investors, for example, refers to ETFs as iShares. Shares that track an S&P index are called SPDRs.

But beyond all of this confusion is a simple way of looking at ETFs. The simplest definition, of course, can be found in its name. An ETF is a fund that trades on an exchange. In other words, it has the format of a mutual fund and the trading structure of a stock. More specifically, when you buy shares in an ETF, you are purchasing a fractional interest in a fund that tracks some type of investment. This can be a commodity, a futures index, or even a basket of stocks. The main thing to keep in mind is that buying shares in an ETF will give you exposure to the underlying investment that it tracks.

What's the Difference between an ETF and a Commodity Index Mutual Fund?

At first glance, ETFs seem quite similar to their mutual fund counterparts. This is especially the case if you compare a commodity index fund with an ETF that tracks a commodity futures index. But aside from their obvious similarities, there are actually some significant differences between the two investment vehicles. More important, these differences alter how you can participate in this commodity bull market.

Stocklike Characteristics

One of the major differences between commodity ETFs and commodity index mutual funds is that ETFs have stocklike characteristics. Now, I know that I mentioned this earlier, but it is important to break down exactly what this means.

Consider, for example, your typical mutual fund and these three characteristics:

1. You typically have to pay a load to enter the fund; there are also yearly expense fees while you are in the fund.
2. Your trading objective is limited strictly to entering or exiting the fund. In other words, you will purchase shares if you are bullish and you will sell shares if you are bearish. Remember that when you do purchase or sell your shares, it has to be at the end of the trading day.
3. Typically you have to invest a minimum amount. In short, the certain restrictions imposed by mutual funds can potentially keep you from being more active in the commodity markets.

In contrast, commodity ETFs are not so restrictive. Besides providing you with the same diversifying benefits as mutual funds, they also provide you with six opportunities. You can:

1. Sell short.
2. Buy on margin.
3. Use options.
4. Buy and sell throughout the day.
5. Use stops, limits, and good-till-canceled orders.
6. Buy only one share.

Selling Short. Let's say that you believe the commodity complex has moved up too far in a short period of time. If you were participating in a mutual fund, you would only have two options. You could either ride out the intermediate sell-off, or you could exit the fund and find another investment. You would have these same options with ETFs, but you would also be able to sell short a certain commodity or commodity index.

When it comes to selling short, there can be differences of opinion. Some investors are not comfortable with selling short; others relish the opportunity. Personally, I feel that short-selling can provide you with another avenue of making money. Furthermore, there will come a time when commodity markets will be extremely overvalued and the market will likely transition into a bear market. At that point, there will also be an opportunity to profit from a downward decline in the commodity markets.

Regardless of your short-selling outlook, the fact remains that having the ability to sell short gives you added an advantage over commodity index mutual funds.

Buying on Margin.   While I don't personally advise buying on margin, you can buy ETFs on margin. Once again, I want to remind you that stock margin is different from futures margin. In futures margins, you borrow money from the brokerage firm, pay interest, and use your current investments as collateral. In essence, this gives you the ability to leverage your investment.

This would give more aggressive investors another opportunity that they would not have if they were simply buying a mutual fund. For instance, if you strongly believe that gold will appreciate significantly over the next several months, you might consider paying single-digit interest in order to experience double-digit gains. Again, this is similar to trading any type of stock on margin. If you have used margin in the past and are comfortable with how it works, this might come across as an advantage.

Using Options.   You can also use options on commodity ETFs. Using options can mean a number of different things for different investors. I will not go into the various option strategies, but the idea here is that using options opens up another level of investing. For instance, if you want to aggressively speculate that gold prices will have a sharp move up within the next couple of months, you can buy options on the gold ETF. If the move does not happen, you will lose your initial investment; if, however, it does happen, there is a chance that you can quickly multiply your initial investment.

Besides using options to speculate, you can also use them to hedge your portfolio. Imagine this scenario. Let's say that you have a sizable position in several different commodity ETFs. At one point, your investments made a remarkable run and appreciated by over 20 percent in less than two months. Given the fact that this move occurred in such a short period of time, you feel that there is a potential for a sharp correction. However, you also do not want to miss a further move up in the markets. In this case, you can spend some money buying put options on the ETFs so that you can hedge your current portfolio holdings. If the price of commodities does decline, you will be able to offset some of your portfolio losses with the gains from your options. Conversely, if the prices keep on climbing, you still will be able to participate in the gains (minus the costs of the put options).

In a way, this is quite similar to corn farmers who want to hedge their sizable crop. You are putting up a small fixed amount to protect your larger portfolio holdings. It goes without saying that you would not have this opportunity if you were investing in a commodity mutual fund.

Buying and Selling Throughout the Day. Another advantage of commodity ETFs is that you have the ability to enter and exit throughout the trading day. As I pointed out, you can purchase or sell shares in mutual funds at the net asset value only once a day. While this might not seem significant if you are a buy-and-hold investor, it is important if you are much more conscious of daily market movements. Often breaking news or financial reports occur during the market hours. The ability to purchase shares of ETFs during the day gives you an added advantage in capitalizing on the positive news or reports.

Similarly, you can also protect yourself if the market moves against you. Most often, major market moves occur during market hours, when investors have the opportunity to react and sell their holdings. In a mutual fund, you would have to wait until the end of the day to sell your shares. As you can imagine, this would put you behind the herd that was selling during the day.

Use of Stops, Limits, and Good-Till-Canceled Orders. Most investors are already familiar with stops, limits, and good-till-canceled (GTC) orders. Using these methods, you can more carefully select the price that you enter and exit your positions. For example, if you feel that the Goldman Sachs Commodity Index will drop back to a certain buy level, you can enter a limit order to purchase the shares at your ideal price. You can also put in stops to limit the downside moves in some of your positions. Of course, you probably learned all of this in Investing 101. However, it is important to point out that ETFs can provide you with a more targeted exposure to the commodity markets. In other words, by using commodity ETF investments you can have a greater input on when to enter or exit the different commodity markets.

Buying Only One Share. While there are undoubtedly several more stocklike characteristics that I have failed to mention, I want to point out one last advantage. Unlike mutual funds, where there is a minimum purchase amount (albeit small in some cases), there is no minimum requirement to purchase shares in an ETF. Conceivably you could purchase only one share. While this scenario might not be realistic, it does open up your ability to spread your investment around. Thus, this ability allows even small investors to further diversify.

Lower Costs

Beyond their stocklike characteristics, ETFs also differ from commodity index mutual funds in that they have a much lower cost of ownership. The first cost when you purchase either fund is a transactional cost. For some mutual funds, the cost is either deferred or established as a back-end load. For other mutual funds, you have to pay an up-front load that sometimes can be as much as 5 percent. With ETFs, the transactional cost is simply what you pay for commission. These days, with online brokerage accounts, your initial up-front cost can fall under $10 a trade.

As you can imagine, having a lower transactional cost provides you with the ability to enter and exit a variety of funds more frequently. This can be advantageous if you want to exit some of your investments for the short term, if you want to switch among different commodity sectors, or if you simply want to actively trade the commodity markets. For buy-and-hold investors, there are still some cost advantages to purchasing an ETF. Because of their structure, ETFs typically have lower expense ratios than index mutual funds.

Tax Efficiency

Commodity ETFs are also more notably tax efficient than their mutual fund counterparts, since they rarely distribute capital gains. When mutual fund companies redeem shares, they typically are forced to sell part of their holdings to come up with the cash. The end result is that they often incur capital gains from their positions that are profitable. In turn, these capital gains are passed down to the shareholders in the form of a distribution. At the end of the year, you will then be forced to pay taxes on your portion of these taxable gains even though you did not exit the fund.

In contrast, because of the way they are structured, ETFs rarely make capital gains distributions. Instead of your shares being redeemed by the mutual fund, you are in essence selling your shares to another investor. Consequently, the fund does not have to sell a portion of its holdings.

Note, however, that you will encounter capital gains distributions when an ETF changes the composition of its index. In order to adjust for the new index, the fund will be forced to sell some positions, which will generate capital gains. Nonetheless, these changes occur infrequently, and the taxes are much lower than if you were part of a mutual fund. If you are interested in learning more about the tax benefits, consult your tax professional privately since every person's tax situation differs.

What Are Your ETF Choices?

Even though I have primarily compared commodity index mutual funds with commodity index ETFs, there are a wide array of ETFs that track a variety of commodity investments. One way of distinguishing between the different ETFs is to break them down in terms of what type of commodity investments they follow. There are four ETF categories:

1. Commodity stock index ETFs
2. Commodity futures index ETFs
3. Single-commodity ETFs
4. Commodity currency ETFs

Commodity Stock Index ETFs

Commodity stock index ETFs track an index that is comprised of different commodity stocks. One of the advantages of these ETFs is that you know exactly which holdings you are purchasing on a daily basis. Natural resource funds, however, only disclose their holdings on a quarterly basis. Commodity stock index ETFs further break down into energy ETFs, mining ETFs, and diversified natural resource ETFs.

Energy ETFs. The following ETFs have diversified energy holdings. In other words, the companies they track range from oil and gas exploration companies, service providers, equipment providers, and a variety of other oil-related companies. The difference between these ETFs is based on which index it follows.

Energy Select Sector SPDR Fund (Symbol: XLE): XLE replicates the total return of the energy select sector, which makes up the S&P 500.

iShares Dow Jones U.S. Energy Sector Index Fund (Symbol: IYE): IYE tracks the Dow Jones Oil and Gas index.

iShares S&P Global Energy Sector Index Fund (Symbol: IXC): The S&P Global Energy Sector.

Vanguard Energy ETF (Symbol: VDE): VDE tracks the performance of the Morgan Stanley Capital International U.S. Investable Market Index.

The following ETFs track energy services stocks:

iShares Dow Jones U.S. Oil Equipment & Services Index Fund (Symbol: IEZ): IEZ replicates the return of the Dow Jones U.S. Oil Equipment & Services Index, which is basically a smaller component of the DJ U.S. Oil and Gas index.

PowerShares Dynamic Oil & Gas Services Portfolio (Symbol: PXJ): PXJ tracks the Dynamic Oil & Gas Intellidex. This index is specifically created by PowerShares and is comprised of oil and gas services companies.

SPDR Oil & Gas Equipment & Services ETF (Symbol: XES): XES tracks the S&P Select Oil & Gas Equipment & Services Index.

Last, the following ETFs focus on oil exploration and production stocks:

iShares Dow Jones U.S. Oil & Gas Exploration & Production Index (Symbol: IEO): IEO also tracks a smaller component of the larger DJ U.S. Oil & Gas Index; however, the component it tracks focuses on oil and gas exploration companies.

PowerShares Dynamic Energy Exploration Production Portfolio (Symbol: PXE): PXE seeks to mirror the Energy Exploration & Production Intellidex Index.

SPDR Oil & Gas Exploration & Production ETFS (Symbol: XOP): XOP replicates the S&P Oil & Gas Exploration & Production Select Industry Index.

Mining ETFs. Mining ETFs are not as common as energy ETFs. However, there will likely be more options within the next couple of years. Buying shares in a mining ETF gives you an exposure to a select group of mining stocks. There are two ETFs here:

Market Vectors Gold Miners ETF (Symbol: GDX): GDX tracks the performance of the companies that make up the American Gold Miners Index. This index is made up of primarily gold and silver mining companies.

SPDR Metals and Mining ETF (Symbol: XME): XME follows the S&P Metals & Mining Select Industry Index. This index is comprised of a more diversified group of mining companies than GDX.

Diversified Natural Resource ETFs. Diversified natural resource ETFs are exchange-traded funds that track an index made up of a diversified group of natural resource companies. Currently some of these ETFs also fall under the basic materials category. That is, these companies will deal with such sectors as forestry and paper, chemicals, and industrial metals.

iShares Dow Jones U.S. Basic Materials Sector Index Fund (Symbol: IYM): IYM tracks the performance of the Dow Jones U.S. Basic Materials Index.

iShares Goldman Sachs Natural Resources Index Fund (Symbol: IGE): IGE mirrors the performance of the Goldman Sachs Natural Resource Sector Index.

The Materials Select Sector SPDR Fund (Symbol: XLB): XLB tracks the total return of the S&P Materials Select Sector Index.

Vanguard Materials ETF (Symbol: VAW): VAW follows the performance of the Morgan Stanley Capital International U.S. Investable Market Materials Index.

Commodity Futures Index ETFs

The following two ETFs are most similar to the commodity index mutual funds mentioned in Chapter 7.

iShares GSCI Commodity-Indexed Trust (Symbol: GSG): GSG attempts to replicate the performance of the GSCI Total Return Index.

PowerShares DB Commodity Index Tracking Fund (Symbol: DBC): DBC tracks the Deutsche Bank Liquid Commodity Index, which is made up of futures contracts on the world's six most widely traded commodities: crude oil, heating oil, gold, aluminum, corn, and wheat.

Single-Commodity ETFs

The following four single-commodity ETFs provide you with a specific exposure in a specific commodity.

iShares COMEX Gold Trust (Symbol: IAU): IAU is virtually identical to StreetTRACKS Gold Trust (GLD). Purchasing shares in IAU provides you with an exposure to gold bullion that the trust holds in vaults.

iShares Silver Trust (Symbol: SLV): SLV tracks the performance of physical silver. One share of SLV represents 10 ounces of silver that is held in a vault. Interestingly enough, when Barclay's first started this ETF, it had to deposit 1.5 million ounces of silver in a trust.

StreetTRACKS Gold Trust (Symbol: GLD): GLD basically tracks the performance of the price of gold bullion. GLD is different from the other three ETFs in this category in that the trust actually holds the physical commodity. Consequently, the shares you purchase represent a fractional interest of gold that the trust holds. These shares trade at one-tenth of the price of gold. In other words, if gold is trading at $620/ounce, the share price hovers at around $62/share.

United States Oil Fund (Symbol: USO): USO tracks the price of West Texas Intermediate (WTI) light, sweet crude oil futures contract that trade on the New York Mercantile Exchange. One share represents a single barrel of crude oil. Hence, if crude oil is trading at $55/barrel, the share price typically trades at near $55/share.

Commodity Currency ETFs

While several ETFs track currencies, only the ones listed here track currencies that fall under the commodity banner.

CurrencyShares Australian Dollar Trust (Symbol: FXA): FXA tracks the price of the Australian dollar in the same manner that FXC tracks the Canadian dollar.

CurrencyShares Canadian Dollar Trust (Symbol: FXC): FXC was created by Rydex to track the price of the Canadian dollar. Purchasing shares in FXC provides you with a fractional interest in a trust that holds Canadian dollars.

Using ETFs to Profit from the Commodity Bull Market

After reading about ETFs, I'm sure that you are convinced about using these funds to profit from the commodity bull market. However, there are several more factors that you should keep in mind.

Follow the Index or Underlying Commodity

If you are looking at purchasing ETFs, you also want to look at the index it tracks. Specifically, you want to look at the makeup of the index, for several reasons. First, doing so ensures that you don't overlap your investments. For example, if you are looking at purchasing the iShares GSCI Commodity-Index Trust, you should be aware that the portfolio has nearly a 70 percent exposure to energy futures. Thus, even though it appears to be a diversified index, it clearly has a majority exposure to the energy index. If you also purchase the United States Oil Fund, you will have overlapping exposure to energy futures. Furthermore, some of these stock indices might track similar companies. Instead of purchasing a double dose, diversify your holdings by buying an ETF that has different access to the commodity market.

Second, focusing on the index will give you an idea of which type of commodity investment you are purchasing. If you already have a portfolio of commodity stocks, you might want to consider ETFs that have an exposure to the futures market or the physical commodity. The exposure to the futures market will give you the noncorrelation that I discussed in Part One of the book.

Construct Your Own Portfolio

Also, you have probably noticed that there is a decent variety of ETFs. This provides you with an opportunity to construct your own manageable portfolio. I want to emphasize the word "manageable," because you don't necessarily have to hold hundreds of stocks and several dozen futures contracts to gain an exposure to multiple levels of this commodity bull market. Imagine, for instance, that your goal is to have a diversified portfolio on multiple levels. You want an exposure across a number of different commodities, to both the stock market and the futures market, and you would prefer to spread your exposure among different companies in the same sector.

In any other circumstance, your portfolio would be composed of hundreds of different positions. Not only would you need a substantial amount of money to accomplish this task, but keeping abreast of the movements of every single position would be extremely difficult and time consuming. With commodity ETFs, you are able to accomplish the same goal with less money and a more manageable approach. How is this done? Well, if you look back at the ETF options, you would be able to diversify with only a handful of positions. For stocks, you can pick up shares of an ETF that tracks a diversified basket of oil and gas stocks, an ETF that tracks the mining sector, and a diversified ETF that tracks some other basic material type companies. For your futures exposure, you can purchase a futures index ETF. Last, you can even add some currency and physical commodity ETFs. All told, you would have created a manageable portfolio.

There Is More to Come

Even though a good number of commodity ETFs have been established over the last couple years, there are more to come. The coming ETFs will have a twofold effect. From a market perspective, the new ETFs will create an added demand, which will ultimately affect the prices of these commodities. In fact, this is already happening. Individuals and corporations that previously might not have had access to the futures markets will be able to participate by purchasing shares of an ETF that trades on a stock exchange. When it comes to the physical gold and silver held in vaults, individuals will not only have an easy way of accumulating an interest in the physical metals, but it will also take supply off an already tight market. In other words, with every purchase made in an ETF the subsequent amount of gold or silver is purchased and stored in the vault. Subsequently, less gold and silver supply on the market will have a positive effect on pricing. As an example, in November 2006, rumors of a platinum ETF sent prices skyrocketing by the biggest one-day move in 20 years. Once these rumors turned out to be false, the price subsequently plummeted to near its previous levels. While the jury is still out on whether there will be platinum ETF (due to its thin supply), this incident still shows the buzz and demand that ETFs can have on the markets.

When it comes to your personal portfolio, the new ETFs will give you more freedom to select from the different commodity markets. Pretty soon additional ETFs will have more specific focuses on subsectors and more individual commodities. Make sure to keep an eye out for these funds.

I also want to point out that there are already some products very similar to ETFs. Exchange-traded notes (ETNs), for instance, have characteristics like ETFs but have different structures. Additionally, the London Stock Exchange has recently listed exchange-traded commodities

(ETCs) that focus on several sector-specific futures indices and individual commodities.

Regardless of the future products, the current ETFs provide investors with one of the better ways of participating and profiting from this commodity bull market. Depending on which ETF you use, you can partake in the noncorrelating aspect of the commodity futures market, experience the diversification of your typical mutual fund, and trade as freely as you would any other stock on an exchange.

Conclusion

Of all the commodity investment vehicles, exchange-traded funds are the newest and most intriguing. Their stocklike characteristics and fundlike qualities can provide you with the benefits of both investment vehicles. In addition, depending on which ETFs you invest in, they can provide you with a diversified and a market-specific approach to the commodity markets.

Part Three

STRATEGIES TO PROFIT FROM THE COMMODITY MARKETS

Chapter 9

Commodity Trading Strategies

Give me six hours to chop down a tree and I will spend the first four sharpening the axe.

—Abraham Lincoln

Now that you know the different ways of participating in this bull market, it is important to know how you can profit from it. Futures, stocks, mutual funds, and exchange-traded futures (ETFs) provide you with the investment vehicles to take advantage of this commodity boom, but the strategies that you implement, the advice that you follow, and the markets that you trade are what ultimately will determine whether you even profit from this bull market. In short, even in the midst of rising commodity prices, it is still possible to lose money. Some of the more common reasons are buying too early, selling too soon, or simply listening to the wrong advice.

While these reasons may come across as a given, they reaffirm the fact that it is important to have a disciplined and well-researched plan in place before you start investing in the commodity markets. Not only will this plan provide you with a road map for navigating through the markets, but it will also enhance your ability to make and maintain long-term profits. This is particularly essential in a market that is volatile and ever changing.

This part of the book focuses on some of the diverse ways that you can navigate through this bull market. In this chapter I look at getting started with the different commodity trading strategies. I also give you my thoughts on the benefits of long-term strategies that can help you capitalize on the long-term commodity trends. Chapter 10 caters to individuals who prefer a more managed approach. Chapter 11 focuses on the advantages to having gold as a part of your investment portfolio. And Chapter 12 is for investors who appreciate some form of third-party assistance. In that chapter I examine the different types of commodity tools that can help you navigate through the commodity markets.

Finding the Right Commodity Trading Strategy

In its simplest form, commodity trading strategies are nothing more than ways that allow you to profit from this commodity bull market. On one level, trading strategies mean how you actually approach the market. What is your exact time frame? Are you going to implement a buy-and-hold strategy? Or are you going to actively trade the commodity markets? What about your method for investing? Are you going to trade futures? Or are you going to rely on natural resource stocks for your market exposure? In a way, this definition of commodity trading strategies pertains to your general approach to the commodity markets.

On another level, commodity strategies refer to the actual methods and strategies that you implement to profit from rising commodity prices. You can determine whether to purchase a commodity in many different ways. Some investors focus strictly on a set of technical indicators. Others review crop reports, economic numbers, supply and demand projections, or other forms of fundamental research.

Importance of Commodity Trading Strategies

Regardless of your strategy, I firmly believe that it is extremely important to have a viable strategy in place before you jump into investing in commodities. In fact, the first step in finding the right commodity trading strategy is actually realizing that you need a strategy. Too many times in my career I have come across investors who lacked a trading strategy. This lack of strategy might not have been as important during times when the market moved in their favor, but it proved detrimental when the market corrected or traded in a more unpredictable manner.

If you consider yourself an investor who typically follows some sort of plan or investment protocol, most likely you are ahead of the game. Commodity markets are really no different from any of the other investment markets. Prices typically are pushed higher by supply and demand factors. Consequently, there is a good chance that you can apply some of the fundamental strategies that currently work for you to the commodity marketplace. This is especially the case if you also focus on technical analysis. A chart is a chart no matter which market it depicts.

In contrast, if you are an investor who typically invests in a haphazard manner, it's vital that you focus on finding a commodity strategy that is suitable for you. There are four reasons why this is so important:

1. A strategy keeps your focus.
2. If you have a strategy, you'll have to do less legwork.
3. A strategy helps you manage risk.
4. It provides you with a basis for when you should enter or exit your trades.

Strategy Keeps Your Focus

With so many different commodity markets, several different investment vehicles, and a wide range of strategies, it helps to be focused on a method for trading. This is important on a couple of different fronts. Having a strategy keeps your investment approach consistent. Jumping back and forth from one strategy to another might yield returns initially, but by chasing returns, you are increasing your risk. Even though there will be times where different strategies or markets might outperform your own style of trading, it is best to remember that you are trading for the longevity of this bull market.

In addition, your strategy will constantly remind you of *your* goals and what *you* are trying to accomplish. If your approach is technically oriented, your focus should be on following your pre-established technical indicators. For instance, if you typically trade the markets from a technical breakout approach, the side-to-side movements should not have an impact on your overall trading strategy. Similarly, if your approach to the oil market is long term and fundamentally based, you should not be too concerned with intermediate-term movements. Why does it matter if the price drops from $70 to $60 a barrel if your fundamental research points to higher oil prices in the long term? It shouldn't, if you are following your long-term, fundamentally oriented strategy. On the flip side, if your strategy is focused on capturing the shorter-term trends in the oil market, it is the long-term factors that become irrelevant. Thus, whatever strategy you implement will dictate which market factors are relevant and which are irrelevant.

> **TIP**
> *Define your purpose.* If you are not investing for the short term, short-term factors might be irrelevant. Instead, focus on what will alter the long-term strategies for your portfolio.

A Strategy Requires Less Legwork

Since your strategy will help you focus on relevant factors, you will save time when staying abreast of the commodity markets. It should go without saying that this book should only be your starting point to learning about the commodity markets. Thus, having a strategy in place will allow you to spend time researching and learning about information that directly benefits how you trade the commodity markets. In a way, this is about the age-old adage that it is better to be great at a few things than it is to be good at a lot of things.

Strategy Helps You Manage Risk

Perhaps one of the more important aspects of utilizing a commodity trading strategy is that it helps you manage risk. No matter what type of commodity trading strategy you implement, you always want to have some type of risk management in place that will protect your capital. How much do you allocate to a specific sector? What's the percentage amount per trade? Where do you put your stop? These are just a few questions that you should have answered before you start implementing any commodity trading strategy. No matter which investment vehicle you use, you do not want to put your money in several trades and end up losing a substantial part of your portfolio in a short time. This point is extremely important if you want to participate in the futures market. Remember, futures are highly leveraged. This is a good thing when the market moves in your favor, but it negatively impacts you when it the market moves in the other direction. Hence, managing your risk is extremely important. If you lack a trading strategy, most likely you also will not have a disciplined risk management approach in place.

Strategy Provides You with a Foundation for When You Should Enter or Exit Your Trades

After finishing this book, I am sure that many of you will have an urge to start investing in the commodities markets right away. While I cannot fault you for your eagerness, it is prudent to have a more calculated approach to entering into these markets. A commodity trading strategy can provide you with a guide of sorts. In fact, the whole point behind a trading strategy is that it helps you determine where prices are heading. If you feel that the price of oil is in an overbought position, you might wait for a pullback before you enter the trade. Likewise, if your research points to a seasonal weakness in the gold sector, you might want to wait a while before you invest.

Once you decide to enter certain markets, it is also important to know when you should exit or close out your positions. Your trading strategy should provide guidance on when you should exit a trade. Some investors might choose to exit a position after a certain profit level has been reached; others might close out a position only after the fundamentals change. Again, each strategy has a different exit point.

All in all, there are probably thousands of different strategies and their variations that you can apply to this commodity bull market. The problem, however, is that not all commodity trading strategies necessarily translate into profits. This is why finding a commodity trading strategy that works is just as important as finding the right commodity investment. In addition, you want to pay attention to the time frame of your strategy. With that said, most of the strategies typically fall in one of two categories:

1. Fundamental analysis
2. Technical analysis

Fundamental versus Technical Analysis

Analyzing the commodity markets from a fundamental or technical approach might often yield the same conclusion, but it ultimately requires different logic or calculations to get to that conclusion. Some people swear by using only technical analysis, while others depend on the fundamentals. My advice regarding this topic is to pick what works for you. I am not about to steer you in one direction or another. I have met many successful traders on both sides of this debate. Of course, you also have the option of implementing certain aspects of both strategies.

Something else that you might consider is to focus on what you might enjoy. I strongly believe that if you are passionate about something, you will likely have greater success. If you like to read research reports or think more from a strategic and long-term outlook, fundamental analysis might work for you. Conversely, if you like looking at charts, volumes, and prices, then technical analysis might work. In either case, there are also times when both the fundamental and technical indicators are on the same page. As an example, both styles of analysis can confirm the commodity bull market of the last several years.

Technical Analysis in the Commodity Markets

Given the fact that this book is focused more on the fundamental aspects of the commodity bull market, I will not spend much time discussing the different types of technical strategies that you can implement. I do, however, want to make a couple of points.

As I mentioned earlier, technical analysis in the commodity markets is truly no different from that in any other financial market. Whether you focus on moving averages, technical breakouts, candlestick patterns, or any number of technical indicators, the strategies that you use to trade those markets can easily be transposed to trade commodity futures, commodity stocks, and commodity ETFs. The basic premise behind technical analysis is simply that the fundamentals are already reflected in the prices. As a result, it is pointless to spend time reviewing reports and other fundamental factors.

Those who prefer to focus on technical analysis often spend time reviewing the price, volume, and pattern and trading of a commodity market over a period of time. By studying these recurring patterns, investors can have an idea of how the markets will trade in the future. This school of thought contains a plethora of different technical trading strategies. If you are interested in learning more, there are several good books on this subject. You can find some listed at www.commoditynewscenter.com.

Fundamental Analysis in the Commodity Markets

As you can tell, my outlook on the commodity markets is heavily centered on fundamental analysis. Most definitions of fundamental analysis describe a process in which you evaluate securities. If you consider a commodity stock, for example, your primary research will be based on its balance sheet, the statistics that result from its data, and any accompanying information regarding the company. As an example, individuals who focus on fundamental analysis will look at the price to earnings ratios, various valuations of the company, the dividend that the company pays, and its general prospects for growth. The idea is that you are trying to find out what makes a company tick and, more important, what the future holds.

In the commodity markets, fundamental analysis focuses simply on the factors that dictate price movements in the physical and futures markets. From a broader sense, this means formulating a strategy that looks at supply and demand factors. More specifically, this means focusing on crop reports, inventory reports, weather, news, and a magnitude of other variables. In other words, you want to stay abreast of any factors that can affect the short-term and intermediate prospects for commodities.

A simple way of keeping track of changing situations is by asking two questions:

1. What can possibly affect the supply of a certain commodity?
2. What can affect the demand for this commodity?

If you think about it, these two questions are at the core of fundamental analysis of the commodity markets. Whatever factors will affect supply or demand will ultimately affect the price of the commodity. When it comes to implementing certain strategies, it is also important to distinguish between the different trading time frames. A record corn crop report (that suddenly pushes prices lower) might initially impact a shorter-term trading strategy, but ultimately it will be insignificant for a longer-term strategy that is focused on longer-term price forecasts. Thus, depending on your time frame, you can implement a variety of different commodity trading strategies. If your focus is short term, then you will have to answer the preceding questions from a short-term outlook. If your focus is long term, the questions must be answered from a long-term outlook.

Weather. Weather is one fundamental factor that can quickly alter the supply situation of certain commodities. Consider the orange juice futures example discussed in Chapter 5. Prior to Hurricane Wilma, the orange juice futures market was expecting a certain amount of oranges for that year's crop. Based on the expected supply, the price of orange juice futures was adequately reflected in the futures market. After the hurricane, it became clear that the weather had destroyed a significant portion of the orange juice crop. The affect on supply quickly translated into higher orange juice futures prices.

Weather often impacts the intermediate supply of most soft commodities. For example, a severe drought in Australia may destroy a substantial amount of its wheat crop, or a tsunami may impact sugar production out of Thailand. In some situations, weather can also affect the energy sector. We clearly saw this when the hurricane season of 2005 damaged refineries and sent oil and natural gas prices to new highs.

While not as widespread across a multitude of commodities, weather can also have an impact on the demand for certain commodities. I am referring to the impact of extreme temperature on the energy sector. If an unexpected cold front hits the East Coast, the demand for heating oil will rise sharply. Similarly, hot temperatures will force many people to crank up their air conditioners. In addition, expectations of future demand or future supply can have just as much of an impact as the actual change in demand and supply. For instance, if most people anticipate a colder winter, typically prices will head higher in anticipation of increased demand. If a colder winter in fact occurs, then the prices will have been correctly forecasted. In contrast, if the weather turns out to be warmer than expected, prices will subsequently fall back down to their previous levels.

How do you trade weather? Unfortunately, you cannot really predict weather accurately. If meteorologists have trouble predicting a five-day forecast, you probably don't stand a chance of accurately predicting future weather patterns. However, while you might not be able to predict upcoming weather accurately, you can speculate on what might happen. If you speculate correctly, you can make money. If you speculate incorrectly, you will likely lose money.

In a more fundamental sense, paying attention to the impact of weather on commodities can help you alter some of your intermediate-term outlooks on the commodity markets. Imagine for a second that based on your fundamental research, you concluded that there would be an oversupply of sugar for the next year. This was reaffirmed by various reports stating that this year's sugar crop would be the largest in over a decade. Subsequently, you decide that it might make sense to enter a short position in the sugar markets. In this scenario, it might make sense to keep tabs on potential weather situations that can alter this outlook. For instance, what would be the impact if a tsunami destroyed a substantial portion of the Southeast Asia sugar crop? Obviously, the projections for a record sugar crop would be altered. Then you might also want to reevaluate your short positions.

News. News is another fundamental factor that can immediately impact supply, demand, and the expectations of supply and demand. Perhaps the most visible example of news affecting the price of certain commodities can be seen with the escalating tensions that have occurred in the Middle East over the last several years. Whenever a news story breaks that takes the geopolitical tensions to another level, the news impacts a couple of different commodities. On the supply front, oil prices typically rise as the fear of war or tensions in the Middle East will result in a drastic decline in oil output. In other words, speculators enter the market anticipating that a war with an oil producing country will curb back supply. This diminished supply will naturally send oil prices rising. On the demand front, the price of gold often rises as demand for a historical safe haven increases.

Another example of news affecting supply and expectations of supply can be seen in several strikes at mining companies over the last several years. As commodity prices have risen, many workers have argued for increased wages and benefits. Workers from the Escondida copper mine in Chile went on strike for 25 days in August 2006. The news of the strike at the world's largest copper mine initially sent prices rising higher for two reasons. First, copper output would be at a standstill while the workers were on strike. Second, the expectations of this strike taking a while to resolve would further decrease copper output. Interestingly enough, as talks about an agreement came to the forefront, copper prices declined.

As you can see, news often has an effect on expectations of supply and demand. Speculators often trade on news in anticipation of a change in potential supply and demand. If their predictions turn out to be correct, then prices will likely stay at those higher levels. However, if the expectations prove to be incorrect, prices will typically fall back down to previous levels.

In addition to providing trading opportunities for more speculative investors, news generally leads the way in terms of providing updated supply and demand outlooks. News reports on China's record gross domestic product growth, India's growing working class, or any number of commodity-related headlines often confirm or deny the potential strength of some commodity markets. In fact, I often give more weight to unbiased news headlines than I do the opinions of many experts. News headlines simply report the facts and allow me to formulate my own opinions about the commodity markets.

Data/Reports. Fundamental data or reports can also provide you with insight on the supply and demand situations for various commodity markets. The Energy and Information Association (EIA) puts out a report that states the demand and supply statistics for energy consumption (including natural gas, oil, heating oil, and unleaded gas). The United States Department of Agriculture (USDA) provides past historical data on agricultural commodities and supply and demand estimates for them. Several other governmental agencies make projections for what the demand and supply situation will be for certain commodities.

In addition to U.S. governmental agencies, independent companies also provide historical data and projections for supply and demand on various commodity markets. For example, Johnson Matthey and GFMS are two companies that provide fundamental data and information on gold, silver, and the platinum group metals. Although these companies provide projections on supply and demand, it is important to keep in mind that they are simply projections.

All in all, a variety of sources provide data and projections on various commodity markets. In addition, trade reports, consumption reports, and general growth reports that governments issue might indirectly impact your intermediate outlook on those markets. Consider, for instance, the GDP growth for China. A report on GDP generally measures the growth rate of the economy. If you look back at the historical GDP growth of China, you will see that it has grown alongside the commodity bull market. As China's economy has expanded, so has the demand for commodities. With a slowing economy, demand for commodities will also decline.

There are a couple of reasons that fundamental data are so significant. First, market participants often rely on these reports for their trading decisions. The significant impact that the U.S. Department of Agriculture corn crop report had on the markets is an obvious example of this. The second reason is that these reports often provide insights on the trends that have occurred and will likely occur in those markets. In turn, this can better equip you to profit from intermediate-term trends that might occur.

Other Fundamental Factors. Besides weather, news, and data reports, other fundamental factors will ultimately impact supply and demand. If you have trouble finding out which of these factors are important, fall back on the questions about what will affect supply and demand for your specific time frame. Most likely this will help you figure out what is important.

Long-Term Strategies for a Long-Term Bull Market

Perhaps the best strategy for this commodity bull market is to realize that we are in a bull market. Once you come to this conclusion, you can profit from rising commodity prices in many different ways. In addition, you can use this long-term outlook as a strategy in itself. Consider for instance these central factors behind the long-term bull market outlook.

- We are still in the early stages of a secular bull market. Even though commodity prices have hit nominal multiyear highs, I fully expect this commodity bull market to last another decade or longer.
- China, India, and other developing economies are at the forefront of why commodity prices are heading higher. Their appetite for raw materials will not subside anytime soon, and I expect this demand to continue as they continue to industrialize.
- An accelerating demand for commodity consumption centers on the fact that one-third of the world's population is getting wealthier, changing their diets, and slowly accumulating goods that are typically associated with western lifestyles.
- In the midst of this growing commodity demand, the supply situation of many commodities is declining, due to the finite nature of commodities and the long-term process for commodity production.
- Nominal prices do not reflect the true price of commodities. When gauging if a commodity has hit an all-time high, it is best to adjust it for inflation. Understanding where the real high for commodities is will give you a better understanding of how far the prices have come and how much more room they have to move.

I bring up these themes for a couple of reasons. The first is that after reviewing the mechanics of how to participate in this bull market, I want to make sure to bring you back to the main topic at hand: We are in the midst of the greatest commodity bull market ever. The factors that are transpiring in front of our eyes not only reaffirm this fact, but they also provide insight on how to profit from this market. This is the second reason that I have outlined the factors that are driving this bull market.

By focusing on these factors, you can better implement strategies to profit from these price moves.

Indeed, one way to approach this bull market is by having a long-term trading strategy that can take advantage of long-term trends. There is no question that there will be months and even years where certain commodity markets might actually decline in value, but by the time this bull market run is over, commodity prices typically will end up at much higher levels. How do I know this? Well, take a look at the central themes of this commodity bull market. The driving forces behind this bull market are far from over. Even after massive industrial expansion in one-third of the world, prices are still cheaper than they were years ago. And to top it all off, the supply situation for most commodities is looking bleak.

In addition to these factors, we also have history as our guide. In most situations, it is difficult to predict the direction of financial markets 10 years out. Economies seem to be constantly changing, and factors can seemingly come up that sway the direction of markets one way or another. Historically, we know that no commodity bull market has lasted less than 15 years. Equally as significant is the fact that increased commodity consumption, whether at an accelerated or a moderate pace, is a foregone conclusion. Based on this knowledge, perhaps the simplest strategy that investors can implement is to capitalize on these long-term trends by holding long-term views through the longevity of this bull market.

Conclusion

Deciding how to profit from this long-term boom is at the center of any commodity trading strategy. For some investors, commodity trading strategies are simply taking a long-term view on a diversified group of commodities. Regardless of where the market moves in the intermediate term, these investors focus on profit from the rising prices that will occur several years down the line. For others, profiting from this bull market is about quickly entering and exiting the various commodity markets using specific technical indicators. If you find yourself in this category, you might value markets that are volatile, since they provide trading opportunities.

Whatever trading method you decide to use, technical or fundamental analysis, you must approach the commodity markets with a purpose, discipline, and strategic focus. Not only will this result in greater insights into the specific markets you decide to trade, but it also provides your portfolio with greater stability.

Chapter 10

A Managed Approach

Managed Futures

There is only one side of the market and it is not the bull side or the bear side, but the right side.

—Jesse Livermore

Some investors prefer a more managed approach to the commodity futures markets than self-directing their investments. While they understand the basic strategies, concepts, and benefits of commodity futures, they would much rather gain access to the futures market through a professional money manager who will monitor their account on a daily basis, come up with the actual trades, and implement the necessary risk management strategies. If you fall in this camp, managed futures can provide you with this opportunity. In addition, managed futures provide *all* investors with an alternative investment that can enhance portfolio returns, lower overall portfolio risk, and even make money in both up and down markets.

In this chapter I introduce an actively managed approach to the commodity markets and to a relatively new asset class that has grown considerably over the last 30 years. I look at the characteristics that make up the managed futures industry, the benefits of managed futures as an asset class, and the pivotal steps that you need to take in order to find the right manager for your portfolio.

Growth of Managed Futures

The term "managed futures" refers to an industry that is made up of professional money managers, known as commodity trading advisors (CTAs), who trade client accounts from a discretionary basis. At first glance, CTAs are similar to mutual fund managers in that they have discretionary authority over what is purchased or sold in your portfolio. Beyond this similarity, CTAs differ in three ways:

1. They transact strictly in the futures markets.
2. They have the ability to use alternative trading strategies (such as writing options or selling short).
3. They have a fee structure that is more heavily based on the performance of client accounts.

As I pointed out in Chapter 2, futures have been trading for several hundred years. Managed futures, however, have only been around for the last several decades. Because of their newness, the managed industry initially attracted only a limited amount of capital. According to Barclay's Trading Group, the amount of money in managed futures in 1980 was $310 million. Over the next 26 years, the flow of money into managed futures has grown significantly. Take a look at Table 10.1.

As you can see, in 2006, the amount of money in managed futures had grown to $170 billion. There are a couple of key reasons for this exponential growth. The first reason has to do with the general growing interest in absolute return strategies. Absolute return strategies can be defined as investment strategies that strive to have positive returns regardless of the performance of the stock market or other benchmarks. In other words, these strategies seek to make money in both up and down markets. In contrast, relative return strategies focus on making money relative to certain benchmarks or indices. Most investors have used relative return strategies. Over the last several years, however, investors have

Table 10.1   Money under Management in Managed Futures, 1980 to 2006

$ Billions on Dec. 31		$ Billions on Dec. 31		$ Billions on Dec. 31	
1980	0.31	1989	7.00	1998	36.00
1981	0.38	1990	10.54	1999	41.30
1982	0.56	1991	14.50	2000	37.90
1983	0.63	1992	18.50	2001	41.30
1984	0.77	1993	26.00	2002	50.94
1985	1.49	1994	24.90	2003	86.50
1986	1.96	1995	22.80	2004	131.90
1987	3.90	1996	23.98	2005	130.60
1988	5.51	1997	33.10	2006	170.00

sought investments that have the ability to make money in any economic circumstance. Managed futures, hedge funds, private equity, and other investments have filled this void.

Trading in managed futures also has grown because they have been around long enough to have a track record. This trading history can serve as a point of reference when comparing portfolios with and without managed futures. Even so, the fact that there has been such an increase in money under management should point to the benefits of allocating a portion of one's portfolio to managed futures.

Benefits of Managed Futures

And indeed, there are benefits to managed futures, ranging from having a professional manage your commodity futures investments to participating in the diversifying qualities of a unique asset class. Take a look at some of these benefits in detail.

Professional Management

One of the most obvious advantages associated with managed futures is that your commodity exposure is fully or partly determined by the trading decisions of a professional money manager. As you might recall from an earlier discussion, this could be a good or bad thing. If the manager is making you money, then it's a good thing. Yet there are many "professional" managers who fail to make money for their investors. The same concept applies to commodity trading advisors. The goal is to find a reputable CTA with a long-term track record. Later I go into more detail about how to select a CTA, but for now, I want to list some of the benefits of professional management.

- *Full-time focus.* The truth of the matter is that average investors have neither the time nor the resources to be fully involved in commodity trading. This does not mean that they cannot be successful trading commodities on their own. However, it does highlight the strengths and advantages of a CTA. CTAs do not have to divide their time among a couple of different jobs. Their primary focus is to make money for their clients. They spend time studying the markets, keeping abreast of any changing or breaking economic news, monitoring client accounts, and basically focusing on one goal: to make clients money.

- *Defined trading strategy.* CTAs also have a defined trading strategy. This is beneficial on a couple of levels. The first is that you know ahead of time what you are investing in before you even invest. Imagine that you wanted to participate in the agricultural market, because you already had exposure to metals and energy through other media. Agricultural CTAs would be the place to start your search. Distinguishing among the managers even further, you would be able to look for those who trade the agricultural markets from a systematic trend-following perspective, managers who use spreads in the agricultural markets, or managers who simply use discretionary decisions based on long-term trading experience on an agricultural exchange. The second benefit of a defined trading strategy is that it allows CTAs to focus on certain markets or strategies that they know really well. Once again, this goes back to what I said earlier: It is best to be great at certain things than good at a lot of things.

- *Money management and risk management in place.* An often-overlooked aspect of trading is money management and risk management. These terms pertain to strategies that investors implement to limit their downside loss and to make their money work for them for the life of their account. Decisions such as where to put the stop, when to get out of a winning trade, and how much money to allocate to a certain trade now fall on the manager. In most cases, CTAs should have strategies in place that have worked successfully for a while.

- *Incentive-based fee structure.* A majority of CTA fees are based on an incentive format. Generally, CTAs charge a management fee (typically around 1 to 2 percent) and a performance/incentive fee (typically around 10 to 20 percent). If the client's account is profitable, the CTA receives more money. If an account is not profitable, the CTA has an incentive to bring it to a profitable level. In summary, this gives the CTA a reason to focus full time on the accounts, stick to defined strategies, and implement effective money management and risk management techniques.

Ability to Make Money in Up or Down Markets

I briefly alluded to the fact that managed futures qualify as an absolute return strategy. When you consider the fact that CTAs are compensated on their performance, this makes perfect sense. In other words, there is no incentive for beating a pre-established benchmark that has negative performance. And this is a good thing. It provides the managers with the motive to come up with trading strategies that can profit in multiple environments. In short, the end goal is to make money regardless of whether the market is moving up, down, or sideways.

This, in fact, is another advantage of managed futures. Unlike other relative performance managers, CTAs have the ability to be long or short in the market, sell call or put options to collect a premium, or implement any other strategies that have the potential to result in absolute return. I elaborate on some of these different types of CTA strategies later, but for now I want to clarify this point.

Let's go back to the agricultural CTA example. Imagine that you decide to invest money with the CTA who trades the agricultural markets from a discretionary basis. This trader has worked in the agricultural industry and has extensive knowledge of the grains markets. Because of this knowledge, she can either sell short or be long wheat futures. That is to say, her knowledge does not pertain only to the long side of the market. She can also use her knowledge to profit from declining prices.

Thus, the manager can profit from whatever direction she thinks prices are heading.

Another example can be seen with an option-writing manager who profits by selling both call and put options that are out of the money. The basic strategy is that the manager believes the options will expire worthless, and he will be able to collect the premium. Since options expire worthless in any economic environment, the manager has the ability (assuming he picks the correct options that expire worthless) to make money regardless of the market conditions.

Potential for Enhanced Portfolio Returns

Understandably, the ability to make money in up or down markets also contributes to a subsequent benefit: Managed futures have the ability to enhance the returns of your portfolio. Consider Figure 10.1, which shows the performance of managed futures (as measured by the Barclay CTA index) versus several worst-case declines for various sectors.

You can clearly see that during some of the worst performance periods for the Standard & Poor's (S&P) 500, managed futures had positive returns. It should probably go without saying that the returns of portfolios that had an allocation to managed futures would have outperformed a peer group strictly invested in the S&P. Several studies have confirmed this point. Here is a summary glimpse of comments from some reports:

Chicago Board of Trade (CBOT). The CBOT conducted a study in which they determined that portfolios made up of 45 percent stocks, 35 percent bonds, and 20 percent managed futures had greater returns and less risk than portfolios that had a 0 percent exposure to managed futures.

Chicago Mercantile Exchange (CME). The CME also concluded: "Portfolios with as much as 20 percent of assets in managed futures yielded up to 50 percent more than a portfolio of stocks and bonds alone."

MAR Managed Futures Study. The study stated: "By allocating about 14 percent of the assets to managed futures, we get a 14.6

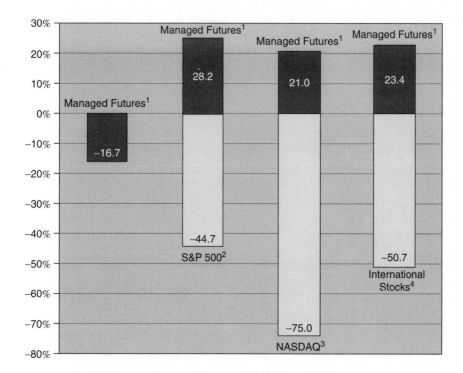

Figure 10.1 Managed Futures versus Worst-Case Declines
SOURCE: Barclay Trading Group, Ltd. and Chicago Board of Trade
[1] Managed Futures: Barclay CTA Index. Greatest drawdown, 6/89 through 10/89.
[2] S&P 500 Total Return Index. Greatest drawdown, 8/00 through 9/02.
[3] NASDAQ Composite Index. Greatest drawdown, 2/02 through 9/02.
[4] International Stocks & Morgan Stanley Capital International Europe, Australasia, and Far East (EAFE) Index. Greatest drawdown, 12/99 through 3/03.

percent reduction in standard deviation. Further, we see that for all available levels of returns in an efficiently-allocated stock/bond portfolio, the inclusion of managed futures lowers the standard deviation—offering better return/risk characteristics."

Center for International Securities and Derivative Market (CISDM). The CISDM department at University of Massachusetts, Amherst, wrote a research paper titled "The Benefits of Managed Futures." In the conclusion, the authors reported that "in contrast to most stock and bond investment vehicles as well as many hedge fund strategies, managed futures offer unique return opportunities which exist through trading a wide variety of global stock and bond futures and options market and through holding either long or short investment positions in different economic environments."

Several other studies have concluded the same thing. In summary, managed futures provide investors with better return/risk characteristics due to their ability to implement a diverse level of strategies while participating in a wide array of markets.

Lower Portfolio Risk

Lower portfolio risk becomes part of the equation when you add an asset class that is not correlated to your typical stock/bond portfolio. This corollary goes back to Henry Markowitz's insights on diversification. As you also can probably conclude from Figure 10.1, having a part of your portfolio in an asset class that was making money would have lowered the general volatility of your portfolio. In other words, the 23 percent decline in the S&P during 1987 would have been softened by a part of your portfolio that would have yielded 21 percent.

Figure 10.2 also clearly shows how adding managed futures to your traditional portfolio can not only enhance the annual compound rate of return, but also lower the annualized standard deviation (risk).

Clearly, there are some undisputable advantages to holding managed futures. Nonetheless, there are several important points to remember. First, just because you have an allocation to managed futures does not mean that your portfolio will always have a higher rate of return and less risk. The studies I mentioned were conducted over a longer period. There were years when managed futures had negative returns or returns that were much less than that of the S&P 500. Additionally, some CTAs have had negative returns even in the years that managed futures were positive.

This, in fact, leads me to the second point to remember. Just because a manager is a CTA does not mean that he or she will have an impressive track record. For every CTA who has a consistent and notable track

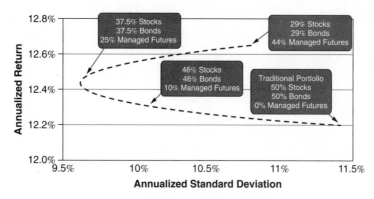

Figure 10.2 Potential Impact of Managed Futures on the Traditional Portfolio, January 1980 to December 2004
SOURCE: Barclay Trading Group, Ltd. and Chicago Board of Trade

record, you will find several more with losing track records or those that are too short to depend on. Thus, it is important to take the time to find a CTA who not only fits your portfolio goals but also has the track record and ability to perform consistently.

A Closer Look at Commodity Trading Advisors

Before you start investing with a CTA, the CTA (or representative) will have to provide you with a disclosure document. The disclosure document (DDOC) provides prospective clients with the necessary information on the managed futures program. Among other things, the DDOC typically outlines the manager's background, his or her trading experience, the track record of the program or programs, the risks associated with the investment, the fees, the markets that the CTA will trade, and the general strategies that will be implemented in your account.

The disclosure document also provides insights on what type of categories the manager falls in. Although CTAs will not specifically tell you how they trade, the information in the DDOC will allow you to distinguish CTAs based on their general trading strategy, markets that they trade, and method of trading.

Trading Strategy

As with individual trading strategies, CTAs typically have certain strategies that they use to generate returns. From a more general perspective, these managers focus on technical analysis, fundamental analysis, or both. Within these categories, trading strategies often evolve into more specific styles. Take a look at some of the following examples.

Trend following. Managers who trade the markets (long and short) from a trend-following perspective enter trades after certain trends have been confirmed. In other words, trend-following strategies do not look to find the bottom or the top, but rather to enter after a trend has already been established.

Countertrend. This strategy is opposite from trend following, in that it seeks to profit from small trades that occur from trend reversals.

Arbitrage. This strategy consists of buying and selling the same commodity on different exchanges. The goal is to profit from the price differentials.

Option writing. Option writing consists of selling options with the purpose of collecting the premium. Within this sector are spread option writers and naked option writers.

Spread trading. There are a variety of different spread trading strategies. The aim is to take advantage of market conditions. This can be done by selling a specific contract month and buying a farther-out contract or by selling a commodity (such as corn) and selling a similar commodity (such as soybeans).

Fundamental focus. This strategy consists simply of focusing on fundamental factors (crop reports, weather, economic reports, etc.) to trade the markets.

Markets Traded

Another factor that differentiates one CTA from another is the markets that they trade. Many CTAs trade primarily financial or currency futures markets. Their trading strategies excel in these highly liquid environments. Since their focus is primarily on implementing technically oriented programs, they want to trade the markets that offer them the most opportunities. As an example, most option-writing managers focus on writing options on the S&P 500. While this is not a bad thing, it does not offer exposure to the commodity markets.

Some managers do transact in the commodity markets. Some focus on energy-specific markets, others focus on agricultural markets, and still others focus on metals. In truth, there are many different combinations of which sectors and which markets CTAs will trade. Some managers even trade a diversified portfolio of commodity markets that span all of the sectors.

Discretionary versus Systematic Trading

CTAs are further characterized by their approach to trading. Discretionary traders are those who ultimately rely on their own (human) decisions for initiating trades. They might use a number of technical and fundamental strategies (and even quantitative programs) to come up with a trade, but ultimately the decision to buy or sell falls on the their shoulders. Systematic traders, however, rely only on computer-generated programs for their trade signals.

Finding the Right CTA for Your Portfolio

Finding the right CTA is like finding any other investment. It takes research, due diligence, and a good bit of legwork. Some managed futures specialists can assist you in this search, or you can go through the process on your own. No matter which path you take, it is best to start by asking yourself three questions.

1. *Which trading strategy do you prefer?*
   The first step is to determine which trading strategy you prefer—or if you even prefer one. Some clients have had specific requests (i.e., trend-following managers only, managers who trade only in the commodity futures markets, etc.), while others were not particular about the strategy as long as the manager had a successful track record. If you do have a strategy or type of CTA that you prefer, it is best to focus specifically on those types of managers. If you care more about

the CTA's track record and the diversifying aspect of managed futures, you can start by scanning the whole managed futures universe.

2. *How much money do you want to invest? (What is your risk capital?)*

The answer to this question is important because many managers have an account minimum requirement. CTA minimums range from $10,000 to $10 million. It would probably not be in your best interest to spend time researching a manager you would not be able to invest with. Moreover, knowing the amount that you are looking to invest can provide you with wisdom on how to allocate the funds. It is always best to have a diversified managed futures portfolio that is spread across several different managers with varying strategies.

Another reason why it is important to know how much money you want to invest is because you should only invest your risk capital. In other words, although you may want to allocate a certain amount of your portfolio to managed futures, allocating all your money to them would not make sense. The reason, of course, has to do with risk. There is risk involved in trading managed futures. If you glance back to Figure 10.2, which shows the different portfolios, you will see that an overexposure to managed futures can actually increase your portfolio risk.

3. *What are your portfolio goals? What is your risk tolerance?*

Many times you will find managers who post stellar returns in a single month. The problem with some of these CTAs, however, is that their returns are predicated on how much risk they are taking. Some of these managers will have above-average returns, but they will also have above-average drawdowns (declines from the high point of the account).

Determining your risk tolerance is extremely important. Are you comfortable with a CTA losing 20 percent in a single month, if he has the potential to make 40 to 60 percent a year? If you are quick to say yes, consider how you would react if your account declined by 20 percent. Would you stick it out? Or would you stop trading and cut your losses?

How much you can tolerate depends on your own goals and risk profile. But the key is to at least have an understanding of what you would like to attain and how much you can take if your account declined.

Evaluating CTAs

Once you have answered these questions, you will most likely have narrowed your search or have provided your managed futures advisor with the groundwork for determining which type of manager you would like in your portfolio. The second part is to evaluate the actual managers from a qualitative and quantitative basis. While there is no sure-fire way to evaluating managers, certain aspects of this process simply make sense.

Performance

Performance is a quantitative measure and often the first level that CTAs must pass. If a CTA's track record is not in line with your expectations, such as desired rate of return or maximum drawdown, then it is pointless to continue evaluating other measures. However, looking at performance often is deceiving. Consider the example in Table 10.2.

While the year-to-date (YTD) return for CTA #1 was more impressive, the manager took on a more substantial amount of risk to come up with those returns. The largest drawdown (from March to May) was −29.7 percent. This is nearly six times more than the drawdown (5 percent) of CTA #2. While the 31.8 percent YTD resulted in substantial gains, some investors would have stopped trading after the drawdown in April or May. Thus, they would not have experienced the gains associated with later months.

Indeed, you can measure CTA performance in many different ways. The first is just by looking at their annual rate of return and the second is focusing on their risk-adjusted rate of return. Since the annual rate of return speaks for itself, here I focus on several different ways of calculating risk-adjusted return.

Table 10.2 CTA Performance

CTA	JAN	FEB	MAR	APR	MAY	JUN	JUL	AUG	SEP	OCT	NOV	DEC	YTD
#1	3.4	6.7	−6.8	−16	−6.9	14.1	4.3	9.0	4.3	8.9	−2.1	12.9	31.8
#2	0.57	2.4	−1.9	3.5	5.6	1.25	−3.8	−1.2	3.5	2.2	0.88	4.3	17.3

Risk-adjusted returns are defined as how much risk a CTA has to take in order to come up with these returns. There are several different risk-adjusted measures; here are a few of the most common.

Calamar ratio. The Calamar ratio is calculated by taking the compound annual rate of return and dividing it by the maximum drawdown in the account. Similar to the Sharpe ratio, a higher Calamar ratio is best.

Sharpe ratio. The Sharpe ratio is calculated by taking the rate of return minus the risk-free rate of return and dividing it by standard deviation. The higher the Sharpe ratio, the better.

Sortino ratio. This measure is similar to the Sharpe ratio, but instead of dividing the return by standard deviation, the return is divided by downside deviation. A higher Sortino ratio is better.

Sterling ratio. Here the compound annual rate of return is divided by the average maximum drawdown minus 10 percent. The higher the Sterling ratio, the better.

The good news is that you will not necessarily have to calculate these ratios when searching for managers. Many of the reporting agencies that track CTA performance will have the calculations available. These measures, however, are essential if you want to compare one CTA against another.

Some other variables to consider when comparing returns are maximum drawdowns and recovery time. The term "maximum drawdown" refers to what the greatest decline in the account was from the peak of the account. The term "recovery time" pertains to how long it took for the account to recover from the drawdown. These two variables are important because they inform investors on the CTA's historical expectations of drawdown. For instance, it is quite possible to start trading with a CTA prior to a drawdown. Having a historical point of reference allows investors to determine whether the drawdown is within reason or it is in uncharted territory.

Just as past results are not a guarantee of future returns, maximum drawdowns do not guarantee that the CTA will not suffer greater drawdowns in the future. Nonetheless, this variable does provide another measure of comparison among CTAs.

Track Record Longevity

Another way to evaluate CTAs is to look at their track record, or how long they have been trading their program. In most situations, it is best to find a CTA who has a track record of at least three to five years. Not only do you have a longer period of performance, but the CTA also has had an opportunity to trade through multiple market environments. Many new CTAs—those with less than three years of trading experience—might get out of the gate quickly and be more aggressive in their trading, which might result in higher drawdowns later.

Yet there are two advantages to investing with newer CTAs. Most new CTAs are focused on proving themselves and attracting capital. As a result, they often post returns that are greater than those of other established managers. Also, as CTAs show consistent performance and have a longer track record, they will start raising their minimum account requirements. For example, CTAs who have a $10 million minimum investment requirement did not have that minimum their first year in business. Thus, investing with a newer CTA might give you exposure to an up-and-coming manager who might eventually raise his or her minimum account requirement.

Manager's Experience Level

Experience pertains not only to the managers' experience since running the program, but also prior to becoming CTAs. As already mentioned, the disclosure document often gives you the biography of the trader or traders involved in the CTA. I have actually come across a CTA with no background in the investment world, a fact that his biography revealed. While this factor might have been irrelevant had he had an established and long track record, it became a glaring red flag since his performance was only a year long.

Still, other CTAs might have long careers in the financial industry but in roles that were ancillary to trading. It is important to evaluate whether what the managers have done in the past is relevant to what they are doing today. You might come across an emerging manager that has been trading as a CTA only for a couple of years but has over 20 years experience trading on the floor of an exchange. Although this manager might be a new CTA, he or she has experience that is more substantial than that of some other CTAs.

Other Factors

There are also other factors that you can use to evaluate CTAs. For instance, you can rely on the services of a managed futures advisor who will add another level of due diligence. As an advisor, I often find that speaking to the manager gives me an added level of insight. In addition, I am also able to monitor the trade activity of the CTA, gauge how the CTA is performing against peers, and generally help with the some of the factors I mentioned previously.

It is also important to note that managers' different strategies can excel in different market environments. For instance, a trend-following CTA typically will do well in a trending market environment. If the market is choppy and range bound, trend followers often incur drawdowns. Yet a range-bound market environment can be ideal for other type of strategies. Consequently, having a diversified managed futures portfolio takes on an added level of importance.

Conclusion

There are two sides to investing in managed futures. The first has to do with relying on a professional money manager to trade in the commodity markets. Since the commodity markets are vast and always changing, a professional manager might provide you with a better way of participating in this bull market. If professional management is your primary goal, it is best to find a CTA who has a similar outlook about this commodity bull market or who has a trading strategy that you appreciate and understand.

The other side to managed futures is that it provides every portfolio with a new and diversifying asset class. This asset class can provide you with an investment that has the potential to enhance your portfolio returns, lower the overall risk of your stock and bond portfolio, and provide you with the opportunity to make money in both up and down market environments.

Chapter 11

The Case for Gold in Your Portfolio

In the absence of the gold standard, there is no way to protect savings from confiscation through inflation. There is no safe store of value.

—Alan Greenspan

Never have the world's moneys been so long cut off from their metallic roots.

—Murray M. Rothbard

Most people do not fully grasp the benefits of gold. For some, it is nothing more than a speculative investment. For many, it is simply jewelry. For others, it is just another commodity that will likely appreciate alongside the other commodities. While all of these interpretations capture certain aspects of gold, they fail to truly explain what makes gold an irreplaceable diversifying asset for any portfolio.

This is one of the main reasons why I have decided to write a chapter devoted to gold. I firmly believe that if most investors understood the different reasons for owning gold and the different economic factors that impact the price of gold, they would not have missed out on the threefold appreciation that has occurred over the last several years. More important, understanding the case for gold now will provide investors with a foundation to take advantage of higher gold prices over the next several years.

The other reason I decided to write a chapter on gold is because gold in itself is a strategy. It can provide investors with a hedge against inflation, a hedge against a declining U.S. dollar, and a safe haven during times of political and economic uncertainty. In addition, because gold has effectively and reliably stored wealth for several thousand years, it is the money of choice for many citizens of emerging economies. Consequently, owning gold also provides investors with a strategy to profit indirectly from the income growth of the citizens of China, India, and other emerging economies.

In this chapter I outline some of the different reasons for owning gold, the different economic factors that affect the price, and the various ways that you can invest in gold. I start by briefly looking at the history of gold; in order to understand the dynamics that affect the gold market today, a working knowledge of gold's history is necessary.

A Brief History of Gold

For many people, the history of gold goes back to the first time they received a gold bracelet, a gold necklace, or gold ring. The true history of gold, however, goes back much farther. There are historical reports of ancient Egyptians forming gold jewelry as early as 3000 B.C. The Bible even has several references about golden altars, golden utensils, gold jewelry, and even golden calves. Suffice it to say, gold has been in existence for several thousand years.

Initially, the demand for gold was due to its beauty, scarcity, and chemical properties. Because of its malleability and luster, gold often was made into jewelry and utensils. It was so beautiful that many books refer to the golden splendor of various objects. Gold, however, was not so abundant that just anyone could own it. In fact, gold's scarcity contributed to its importance. Eventually gold became so widely cherished that it became an integral part of international trade. Merchants from one nation could purchase goods from another nation simply by paying with the highly desired gold. In short, the transition from barter to money had started to take shape.

Gold as Money

This transition eventually led to Lydian merchants (in present-day Turkey) to start producing the first gold-based coin around 640 B.C. Instead of measuring gold to verify its accuracy, the coins were created with the purpose of being standardized in weight, composition, and authenticity. (The coins were stamped with a seal.) At first, the coins were made up of a 63 percent gold and 27 percent silver mixture (known as electrum). Later the Lydians began minting coins that were made of only gold or only silver.

As you can imagine, gold as money provided new opportunities for Lydian merchants. Not only had they established an easily transferable form of money (gold was not perishable, easily storable, and soon to be widely accepted), but they were able to expand their economic infrastructure. Instead of trading goods and services for other goods and services, merchants were now able to use the gold coins. This propelled them to establish the first centralized marketplace. A person could sell goods, receive payment in gold, and then walk to other merchants and purchase goods.

Throughout history, gold continued to grow in importance and influence. Greek and Roman empires were able to prosper and expand their economic systems by having a standardized and recognizable currency all across their wide empires. Gold was used to facilitate trade with the Indian spice traders and Chinese silk merchants. In 1066 Great Britain introduced its own metals-based currency (pounds, shillings, and pence). At that time, a pound truly meant a pound of sterling silver. Over the next several hundred years, Great Britain transitioned into using a monetary system that was based on gold and silver.

All the while, the demand for and popularity of gold grew widely. Since gold now unequivocally represented wealth, battles, expeditions, and plunders revolved around accumulating gold. In Asia, Europe, Africa, and the Americas, gold represented wealth.

Gold in the United States

In the United States, gold's history began in 1792, when the bimetallic standard was selected as the nation's currency. This meant that every monetary unit was backed by either a certain amount of gold or a certain amount of silver. In the case of the U.S. dollar, one dollar was equivalent to 24.75 grains of gold and 371.25 grains of silver. This represented a 15 to 1 silver to gold ratio. At the time, you could take gold or silver bullion to the U.S. mint and receive coins that represented the exact value that you brought in. You could then place these coins into circulation and have them represent the gold or silver bullion you deposited with the mint.

It was not until 45 years later that the amount of gold that a dollar represented changed. This was an early version of inflation. Instead of one dollar equaling 24.75 grains of gold, it now equaled 23.22 grains. Another way of looking at it is that an ounce of gold was now trading at $20.67. In 1913 the U.S. monetary system took another turn when the Federal Reserve (the Fed) was established. The Federal Reserve replaced the prior banking system and they begin issuing promissory notes in the form of paper. When issued, these notes stated that they would be redeemed in gold on demand.

The Gold Reserve Act of 1934 was the next milestone in gold's history in the United States. Not only did the act once again devalue the purchasing power of the dollar (you would now have to pay $35 to control one ounce of gold), but it also gave the government two extraordinary powers: It gave the U.S. government permanent title to all the gold coins in circulation, and it put an end to the minting of gold coins. Thus began the transition from gold coins to paper money (as we know it today). For the next several decades, several other and edicts slowly bled gold out of the U.S. monetary system.

The culmination came when the gold standard (where deposits and notes could be converted into gold) was abandoned altogether with the abolishment of the Bretton Woods agreement in 1971. In 1973 the U.S. dollar was officially devalued one last time, when it took $42.22 to purchase an ounce of gold. Eventually gold was able to trade freely in the open markets, and the dollar was backed strictly by the word of the federal government.

What Happened?

The obvious question that should come to your mind after reading this brief history on gold is: What happened? How could thousands of years of monetary history be abolished in less than 40 years? In other words, if gold (in some form or manner) has served as money since ancient times, why is this no longer the case? Or is it?

In response to this question, some people will argue that "things are different now." The gist of the argument is that gold is an archaic or barbaric relic. Economies have evolved, and using gold as money is obsolete. The Federal Reserve and other central banks are now responsible for creating money. Furthermore, even if you wanted to, you could not use gold to buy groceries, pay your mortgage, or for daily transactions. Thus, while gold served as money for a good part of history, it is no longer valid in today's advanced economic age.

But if this is truly the case, why are central banks from all over the world converting more and more of their U.S. dollar reserves into gold? Why does the U.S. government have the world's largest gold reserve? Why are citizens in China, India, and even in the United States converting their local currencies into gold? The short answer to these questions is that even in this advanced economic age, gold is still valid, because it is money and it represents wealth.

Gold Is Still Money

The word "money" is defined as a medium of exchange that is able to preserve wealth. A "medium of exchange" is simply something that is widely accepted to have a certain value and that can be exchanged for goods or services. The U.S. dollar, for example, is a medium of exchange. You can easily transfer the dollar to other individuals because it represents a certain value that will allow you to purchase food, clothing, or a variety of goods and services. The same is true about gold. While you cannot use gold to purchase some of these goods and services directly, you still can use it to purchase dollars or any other currency. Then you can use the dollars to purchase your goods.

Consider, for instance, this scenario. Every month I get paid. In return for my time and labor, I receive U.S. dollars, which provide me with the value necessary to pay my bills and any other expenses. Once I receive the money, instead of putting it in the bank, I decide to go to the local coin shop and purchase some gold coins. Now let's assume that a year later, I decide to purchase a new car. I will then take the gold coins to the local dealer, convert them to U.S. dollars, and take the dollars to the dealership where I can purchase my vehicle. In this case, did gold serve as a medium of exchange? Of course it did.

Now, if gold was not widely accepted and I had difficulty converting it into a local currency, things might be different. However, this is not the case. If I were to purchase gold in Newport Beach, California, get on an airplane, and fly almost anywhere in the world, I would most likely be able to find a jewelry store, a bank, a coin shop, or even a local resident that would be able to easily convert the gold into the local currency. Why would they do this? Well, because they understand that gold is money and it represents wealth.

More important than the fact that gold represents wealth is the fact that gold *preserves* wealth. This is the second part of the definition of money. If you recollect the brief history of gold, the price associated with an ounce of gold has changed considerably over the last several hundred years. In 1837 one ounce of gold was priced at $20.67; in 1934 it was priced at $35; in 1973 it was priced at $42.22; and in 2006 it hit a high of $720. The general trend has been higher gold prices over a prolonged period of time.

This point might not seem extremely relevant when you look at things from a short-term perspective, but it is extremely relevant if you are concerned with preserving wealth. Consider, for instance, the option to purchase an ounce of gold in 1973. The amount that you had to pay was $42.22. At that time, you could spend the $42.22 and purchase an ounce of gold, or you could simply hold on to the money. The difference between the two options is pretty substantial. In 1973 $42.22 could buy a lot more than it could buy today. Today it might be able to purchase a dinner for two at a local restaurant. In contrast, you would have been able to convert an ounce of gold to $720. This amount would be equivalent to 16 dinner-for-two meals or enough money to buy some higher-priced items. Even more significant is that this amount would more clearly represent the wealth that you had accumulated in 1973. By holding on to an ounce of gold, you were able to preserve the value of your wealth. Unfortunately, the same could not be said had you simply kept the $42.22.

Gold Aversion

Even so, the argument that gold is money and that it represents wealth fails to convince many people. For most people, the money that they have in the bank, the home that they own, and the stocks that they hold in their portfolio represent wealth. Furthermore, why would you need to go through all the trouble and hassle of converting gold into dollars if you could simply hold dollars in the first place? Indeed, these mind-sets are pretty prevalent.

> **Tip**
> *Think like a contrarian.* Oftentimes, going against the herd may yield the best results.

I have also come to find that many investors simply are averse to gold. In fact, I am constantly surprised about how adamant some investors are about *not* owning gold. Several years ago I met one such man after I had given a talk on the fundamental reasons for owning gold. Immediately after my presentation, he walked up to me and passionately began telling me he would not buy gold again if his life depended on it. When I asked him why, he proceeded to tell me that he had purchased gold at over $800/ounce in the early 1980s and that he has been waiting for the price to get back to that level ever since. He went on to say that it was the worst investment that he ever made and that he couldn't understand why anyone would want to buy gold.

Since my presentation obviously had no impact on his viewpoint, I did not bother to explain to him why I believed that buying gold at the speculative top is substantially different from owning gold for its underlying qualities. Instead, I just wished him the best of luck and thanked him for coming to my presentation. Later on I realized that while non–gold investors might vary in their reasons for not owning gold, it all comes down to certain factors clouding the obvious benefits of gold ownership. In the case of this man, he couldn't get over the fact that he purchased gold at $800 an ounce and had spent more than two decades waiting for the price appreciate.

What about you? Why haven't you owned gold? Before I continue with the reasons for owning gold, I want to address some potential explanations for why investors have failed to participate in the current gold bull market. As I have pointed out, some people are unable to get over their reasons for not owning gold, even after I clearly explain the benefits. Yet regardless of your success or wealth, owning gold still makes sense. In other words, gold makes sense as both an investment for appreciation and an asset for diversification.

A couple of years ago, in response to a growing disinterest in gold from investors, I decided to list several different potential motives in my newsletter as to why investors were hesitant to buy gold. While these examples are meant to be somewhat humorous, they nonetheless represent the mind-set of a good portion of investors. In fact, I have actually heard these reasons, in some variation or another, from investors. It is also interesting to note that now several of these investors no longer seem as confident.

Real estate–focused investor. Do you know how much money I've made in the real estate market? Not only have my condos appreciated in value, but I have rental income coming in. Why would I want to sell a portion of my real estate and buy gold? Any additional money that I receive, I'll use to buy another condo! As a matter of fact, I don't even need a down payment! I can just get one of those zero-down, interest-only loans!

Stock market fan. The stock market is hot! Corporate earnings, consumer confidence numbers, and a strong economy are driving this market. Why would I want to shift my investments from an earnings-driven equity market to a gold market centered on speculation?

Disgruntled historian. Don't tell me about gold. I still own the gold that I bought when it was trading at over $800/ounce. If I could break even, I'd be a happy camper!

Data-dependent statistician. How can you tell me to buy gold because of rising inflation? Last time I checked, the core Consumer Price Index is minimal, long-term bond yields have remained low, and the Fed has reassured me that inflation is in check. I simply do not see any statistical data that can back your case.

I-have-enough-money-to-last-a-lifetime-so-I-could-care-less investor. I don't need gold. Even if gold prices appreciated considerably, I could care less. I have enough money to last two lifetimes! My advisor recommends treasuries, and that's good enough for me!

Frozen-in-time-machine investor. What's the point? I've already missed the boat. I've been meaning to buy gold for the last several years, but since it has already tripled in value, it's pointless.

Six Reasons to Own Gold in Your Portfolio

Whether you subscribe to the economic outlooks just described, owning gold in your portfolio still makes sense. Consider six advantages that gold can bring your portfolio:

1. It preserves your wealth.
2. It is an alternate to fiat currency.
3. Gold serves as a long-term inflation hedge.
4. It is a hedge against a declining U.S. dollar.
5. Gold is a safe haven during times of political and economic uncertainty.
6. It is a diversifying asset for your portfolio.

Gold as a Wealth Preserver

The first reason, of course, has to do with gold preserving your wealth. No other form of money has stored wealth successfully for such a long period of time. If you are concerned about maintaining your wealth for generations, gold will likely provide you with the most reliable way of accomplishing this. It has withstood scores of generations, several different empires, and countless periods of war and peace. Even if you are more concerned with having enough money for retirement, gold still serves a way to protect your wealth.

Gold as an Alternative to Fiat Currency

Unfortunately, fiat currency does not serve as a way to protect your wealth. Fiat currency is money that is backed strictly by the decree (or declaratory fiat) of the government. The U.S. dollar, the euro, the British pound, and most of the paper money in the world today are fiat money. With fiat money, governments have the power and authority to print more money (increase the supply of money in circulation) as they deem fit.

As you can imagine, governments often have abused their power to print money. Perhaps the most glaring example occurred in Germany in 1923. In the aftermath of World War I, the government attempted to restructure the economy by printing money. The problem was that it kept on printing. The result was hyperinflation, where citizens had to use wheelbarrows of money to buy a loaf of bread. Individuals who once hoped to pass their wealth down to generations were shocked to find out that it could now only buy a loaf of bread.

" 'My father was a lawyer,' says Walter Levy, an internationally known German-born oil consultant in New York, 'and he had taken out an insurance policy in 1903, and every month he had made the payments faithfully. It was a 20-year policy, and when it came due, he cashed it in and bought a single loaf of bread.' The Berlin publisher Leopold Ullstein wrote that an American visitor tipped the family cook one dollar. The family convened, and it was decided that a trust fund should be set up in a Berlin bank with the cook as beneficiary, the bank to administer and invest the dollar."

While this situation was undoubtedly extreme, it still paints the picture of fiat money at work. At any given moment, the government can crank out the printing press, send more money floating around, and quickly erode the purchasing power of your money. With gold, governments don't have this option. Gold is finite, scarce, and quite simply cannot be duplicated by a simple government decree.

Gold as a Long-Term Inflation Hedge

Not surprisingly, gold serves as a hedge against inflation. In other words, during times of inflationary pressures, gold has historically appreciated in value. Another way of looking at this is that during times when fiat money has lost purchasing power, gold has appreciated in value. This makes sense on a couple of different levels. First, once investors perceive that the purchasing power of their dollar, pound, or other currency is eroding, they start shifting their wealth into an asset that has retained wealth for thousands of years. This increased demand for gold will push prices higher. Additionally, inflation is a by-product of an increase in the money supply, or the printing of more money. Thus, if there is now more money chasing the same amount of gold, the price of gold will increase to reflect the true dollar worth.

A recent example can be seen with the inflationary environment of the 1970s. During the 1960s and 1970s, the U.S. government had to spend a good amount of money on the war in Vietnam, the race to the moon, and other costly ventures. One way that the government did this was by printing more money. If this sounds ridiculous, take a look at Figure 11.1, which measures the growth of M3 from 1959 to 1980. (M3 measures the supply of money.)

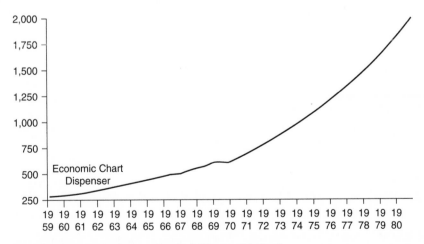

Figure 11.1   M3 Money Stock (billions of dollars)
Source: Economagic, LLC

As you can see, the amount of money that was printed grew exponentially over this time period. The increase in money supply ultimately resulted in a double digit inflation. In response, gold prices appreciated significantly. At the start of the 1970s, gold prices were trading at under $50 an ounce, and they ended the decade trading at over $500 an ounce. The net increase was greater than 1,000 percent.

Thus, if you are concerned about inflation, or at least want to protect your portfolio against the erosion of inflation, having an allocation of gold in your portfolio makes sense. Even during times of low inflation, gold can serve as a form of insurance in case the government decides to start printing more money. In fact, one other related advantage of gold is that it has historically acted as a leading indicator for inflation. In other words, gold prices typically rise before inflation is seen in higher goods and services.

Gold as a Hedge against a Declining U.S. Dollar

Gold is also a hedge against a decline in the U.S. dollar. This has to do with the fact that gold is priced globally in U.S. dollars. Since gold is priced in U.S. dollars, investors have to sell dollars in order to purchase gold. This is especially relevant and significant when central banks state that they are looking at buying more gold and diversifying out of their U.S. dollar reserves. The sale of U.S. dollars will bring further selling pressure on the dollar and accelerate its decline.

Consequently, a declining U.S. dollar would make gold cheaper for investors who are outside of the United States. In turn, this would increase the demand for gold from investors whose currencies have appreciated relative to the U.S. dollar. You can see this inverse relationship with gold and the U.S. dollar in Figure 11.2.

As you can see, even though there have been short time frames where gold and the U.S. dollar moved in the same direction (2005 is an example), over the longer term, gold is an effective hedge against a declining U.S. dollar. Similarly, a strong U.S. dollar does not bode well for the price of gold.

Gold as a Safe Haven during Times of Uncertainty

Whenever situations arise that threaten the stability of a government, an economy, or the purchasing power of a currency, investors start selling

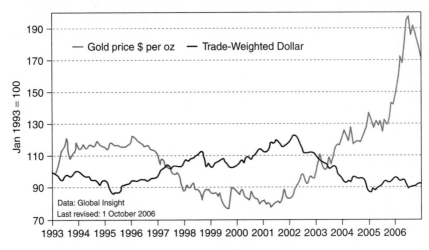

Figure 11.2   Gold and Trade-Weighted Dollar
SOURCE: World Gold Council and *Global Insight*

their currencies and start buying a real asset that historically has been recognized as a safe haven. Why do they do this? Because they are unsure of what might happen in the future. As history has shown time and time again, situations can arise that can jeopardize the stability of a country and its economy. Thus, buying gold acts as insurance in case things do go wrong. And, as history has also proven, political and economic situations often do go wrong. Currencies can collapse, governments can fail, and war can break out at any given moment.

This is why gold buying typically increases during times of crisis. Investors are quick to recall that political and economic instability can erode their wealth. Of course, so are speculators. This is why you often see gold prices spike in response to news about North Korea launching a rocket, a potential crisis in the Middle East, or any event that can result in economic uncertainty.

Gold as a Diversifying Asset

All told, gold provides you with yet another diversifying asset for your portfolio. Several of the factors I mentioned are advantageous for the price of gold but are disadvantageous to other investments in your portfolio. For instance, inflation is positive for the price of gold but is negative for cash, bonds, and dollar–based investments. As a result, having gold can provide you with an asset that will balance out your overall portfolio. In short, gold is not correlated with stocks, bonds, and real estate.

Why Own Gold *Now?*

If you consider some of the reasons I mentioned for owning gold, they are centered on a couple of major points. The first is that gold can help preserve your wealth, and the second is that gold acts as a form of insurance for your portfolio. If the dollar declines, then gold prices will rise and serve as a hedge against the declining dollar. If inflation rises, then gold prices will rise and serve as an inflation hedge. If global political or economic instability arise, gold prices will rise as investor demand for a safe haven grows. Naturally, there will also be periods where inflation will be on the decline, the dollar will appreciate, and geopolitical uncertainty is not on the minds of investors. If that is the case, does it still make sense to own gold? The answer to that question is similar to the answer you would give to a person who asks if it makes sense to have car insurance or fire insurance. Of course it does.

But beyond the fact that gold serves as insurance for certain economic events, acts as a diversifying asset, and reliably stores wealth, gold is also an asset that will appreciate substantially over the next several years. Why do I say this? The same factors that I mentioned as affecting the price of gold are the ultimate reasons why gold has increased over the last few years and why it will continue to do so over the next several years. Consider the current economic landscape of rising inflation, a declining U.S. dollar, continued global instability, and growing investment demand for gold in the midst of declining supply.

Rising Inflation

With the Fed printing money like it was in the summer of 1969, it should come as no surprise that inflation has increased to a level that is above Ben Bernanke's comfort level. Nonetheless, the debate has raged as to on whether inflation is truly a concern. At the core of this debate is the definition of the word "inflation." Most economists, and the Fed, subscribe to the belief that inflation is measured by the rise in the price of goods and services. As a result, they look at the Consumer Price Index (core CPI), which tracks the change of consumer prices for a basket of goods and services, as a gauge for inflation. (More accurately, the Fed prefers to use the core CPI, which excludes food and energy prices).

Other economists argue that higher prices do not cause inflation but are a by-product of an inflated money supply. In other words, higher prices will naturally result when too much money chases too few goods. Of course, I agree with this analysis. Focusing on the price of goods and services as a gauge for inflation is similar to waiting for your kid's report card to find out whether he has failed the class. If you had focused on the fact that he was skipping school or not doing his homework, you might have been able to keep him from failing.

Likewise, focusing on the root cause of inflation will provide you with the opportunity to prepare for the loss of purchasing power. If you look at the current situation, you will notice that the money supply has risen in a similar exponential manner to what it did in the 1970s. The rationale for the increase in the money supply has been to spend money financing a number of unforeseen expenditures, such as the wars in Afghanistan and Iraq. The end result, of course, will be higher prices across the board.

For now, however, the Fed has focused on the core CPI as the gauge for inflation. While the core CPI has risen considerably over the last several years, it still has not captured the true inflation rate. Additionally, the gauge that the Fed uses to measure inflation fails on a couple of different levels. First, it does not take into account the rise in food and energy prices, which are obviously a big part of our spending. Second, it fails to realize that it typically takes a while for higher energy and raw materials costs to trickle down into higher core prices.

I believe that once the higher commodity prices finally pass through to consumer prices and inflation becomes more statistically obvious, there will be another round of buying as investors rush to gold.

Declining U.S. Dollar

The decline in the U.S. dollar is another reason that gold prices have appreciated to multiyear highs over the last several years. Take a look at Figure 11.3. The growing trade deficit and current account deficit

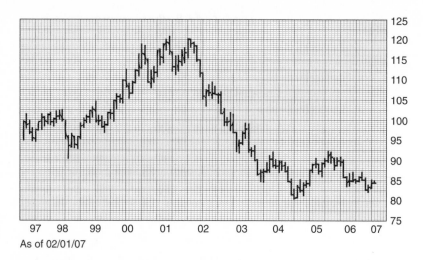

As of 02/01/07

Figure 11.3   U.S. Dollar Index (monthly)
SOURCE: Barchart.com

make it less and less likely that central banks will continue to hold on to such a large amount of U.S. dollars in their reserves. Already China, the United Arab Emirates, Russia, and a number of other central banks have vocally expressed interest in diversifying out of their dollar reserves. I expect this trend to continue as the dollar resumes its bearish decline in the face of growing deficits. Undoubtedly, gold will be one of the major beneficiaries to the central bank's selling off of their dollars.

Continued Global Instability

There is no question that we have seen a growing level of instability and uncertainty over the last several years. Iraq, Iran, Afghanistan, North Korea, Nigeria, and Venezuela are just a few countries that have contributed to global tensions and economic uncertainty. In addition, potential problems, such as avian flu, terrorist attacks, and political coups have seemed to increase in the last several years. All of these factors have created a global environment of uncertainty.

As such, the demand for gold as a safe haven has also increased and will continue to do so, as there seems to be no end in sight for global instability.

Growing Investment Demand for Gold in the Midst of Declining Supply

In addition to the factors that have historically pushed up the price of gold, I expect gold prices to increase due to demand from the citizens of emerging countries. For many of these citizens, it makes perfect sense to own gold. Gold has symbolized wealth for generations and is also a part of their culture. India, for instance, typically experiences an increased demand for jewelry during its festival and wedding season. In China, citizens have only recently been allowed to purchase gold as an investment.

It is interesting to note that even as the price of gold has increased, demand from Asia has continued to grow. In 2006, for example, demand for gold from India grew by more than 10 percent over the previous year, even though the price of gold had moved up considerably. In light of continually higher prices, I expect gold demand to continue rise as citizens in China, India, and other emerging economies amass more wealth.

Coupled with rising gold demand is the fact that gold supply has declined over the last several years. In fact, some economists argue that gold production has reached a peak. Figure 11.4 shows world gold mine production between 1980 and 2005.

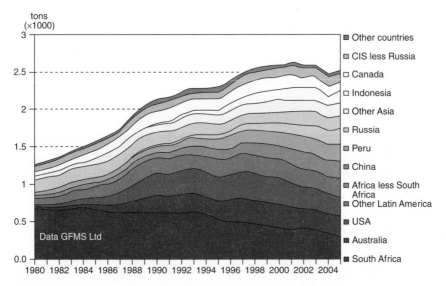

Figure 11.4 World Gold Mine Production, 1980 to 2005
DATA: World Gold Council and GFMS Ltd.

Different Ways of Buying Gold

I hope that by now you understand why it is so important to have an allocation toward gold in your portfolio. Not only does it make sense from a portfolio diversification perspective, but it also makes sense as an asset that appreciates, given the present economic environment. Going forward, I fully expect the price of gold to hit new record highs throughout the length of this bull market.

There are many different ways that you can participate in this gold bull market. Because of gold's role as money, there are actually many more ways to own gold than there are for other commodities. Here are some of the ways that you can capture an exposure to gold:

- Gold futures
- Gold mining shares
- Gold ETFs
- Gold mutual funds
- Gold coins
- Gold bullion
- Gold certificates
- E-gold
- Jewelry

What's Better?

In the same way that there is a debate about whether you should buy gold, there is a debate within the gold community on what is the best way to purchase it. While I will not say that one way is better than the other, I can say that there are certain advantages and disadvantages associated with the various gold vehicles. For instance, gold futures provide investors with the opportunity to leverage their gold investment. Physical gold, such as coins and bullion, provide investors with the comfort of actually knowing that they have gold. In turn, gold certificates and e-gold provide investors with the benefits and entitlement to gold, but with the peace of mind that they do not have to worry about storing it.

If you are more concerned with geopolitical tensions and the need to have access to gold within a short period of time, physical gold will most likely make the most sense. If you don't want to worry about physically owning gold but are primarily interested in profiting from higher gold prices, owning any of the other nonphysical investments might make just as much sense. Last, if you are like my wife, Kelly, gold jewelry might be your investment of choice. In short, deciding on how to gain exposure to gold for your portfolio will also depend on what you are looking at accomplishing. But one thing is certain: Gold is an asset that should be considered for every portfolio.

Chapter 12

Leveraging Third-Party Assistance

If the eye does not want to see, neither light nor glasses will help.

—German Proverb

In the last decade or so, with the advent of the Internet and technology, third-party assistance has grown into a category all by itself. Previously, commodity investors had only a couple major options when it came to their investment decisions: They could either come up with their own trade recommendations based on research and trading strategies, or they could rely on local brokers for trade advice and prudent portfolio management. Today these options include Internet advisory newsletters, Web sites, trading systems, access to specialized brokers all across the country, and a variety of other trading tools and services.

Unfortunately, as great as some of these sources are in providing investors with assistance, they can also lead many investors along the wrong investment path. In particular, many brokers, Web sites, and advisory newsletters have either failed to mention or adamantly opposed this first stage of the commodity bull market. Relying on these sources for assistance would naturally lead you to miss out on the substantial moves that have occurred in the commodity markets over the last several years. Consequently, it is important to find third-party sources that are not only aligned with your investment views, but also do a good job of executing these views profitably.

This chapter serves to direct you to some of the different tools and services that can help you along the way of this long-term commodity boom. It also highlights some of the questions and factors that you should consider before selecting the most appropriate third-party help. While this book has undoubtedly answered many of your questions about the commodity markets, it should also have raised many others. The sources discussed in this chapter can answer some of your questions or guide you to clarification.

Advisory Newsletters

The first source of third-party assistance is advisory newsletters. Advisory newsletters are not really new, but they have grown in size and popularity over the last several years. You might have even received a sample newsletter in your mail or e-mail box. Some of these newsletters will often advertise how much money they have made their clients or even offer a teaser about an investment. The marketing goal is for you to sign up for the newsletter.

Once you sign up, you pay the newsletter publisher a monthly, quarterly, or yearly subscription fee. In return, the newsletter typically provides you with specific trade recommendations, a model portfolio, or macro outlooks on the economy and specific markets. You pay a monthly or yearly subscription fee to access advice and research that is compiled by an independent individual or firm.

Indeed, this is the main advantage to using a newsletter as a form of assistance. Often newsletters will provide specific recommendations and research that will allow you to make better investment decisions. For instance, if you are interested in purchasing an energy-related company because of your bullish outlook on oil, newsletters might recommend a couple of companies that are undervalued in relation to their peers. The newsletters also will most likely expand on reasons for this undervaluation and provide concise company reports. Newsletters also will tell you when you should get out of the investment. Thus, by subscribing, you not only save time, you will also receive guidance and learn about potential valuable investments.

Search Process

The first step in searching for advisory newsletters is simply to differentiate between newsletters that offer sincere recommendations and those that are simply "tout" machines. Tout machines are newsletters compiled by marketing firms with the sole purpose of generating interest and creating liquidity so that insiders can get their shares out. In other words, the recommendations of tout machines are not legitimate, and sometimes, the companies are on their last leg. In many cases, the newsletter contains a disclosure stating that the newsletter marketing company will receive a certain amount of shares in return for marketing the company. However, this disclaimer does not always appear.

Some newsletters do not even disclose that they are representing the recommended company or that they are getting compensated in any way. Thus, you have to look out for other red flags. One obvious way is to look closely at the company that is being recommended. If you do some follow-up research, most likely you will find that the company is trading for pennies and has little or no volume. The immediate question that should arise is: Why is the company is trading for pennies if it's so great? You will also likely notice that the volume of shares traded will increase dramatically during the period that you receive the newsletter. This is because there are a lot more people, just like you, who received the same "hot tip."

Also beware of companies that claim you can make an astronomical amount of money with little risk or that the company is a "sure thing." There is risk in almost every investment, and there is no such thing as sure thing. Last, ask yourself this simple question: Why would someone want to give me a free investment tip? If the company was going to explode toward the upside, wouldn't they keep that to themselves? In all honesty, it is not too difficult to spot these types of tout newsletters.

Once you have figured out which are legitimate newsletters and which are not, you can move on to the newsletters that require a subscription fee. As I stated earlier, these newsletters typically are not compensated for making recommendations; rather, they are compensated by reader subscription fees. In fact, some newsletter writers pledge that they will not participate in the recommendations they make. This establishes a certain level of credibility, where you don't have to be worried that they are simply touting a recommendation. Nonetheless, it is often difficult to prove that they in fact do not participate in the recommendations.

The next step is to find advisory newsletters that can provide you with accurate and profitable information. The sections that follow show you how to narrow your search.

Search by Category. Just as there are many types of advisor-based funds, there are also many different types of advisory newsletters. Area of expertise (markets they follow), time frame of their recommendations, and the investment vehicles that they use are some ways that you can categorize these newsletters. Moreover, you can ask the newsletter editor these questions to gain a better understanding of their makeup and how they might differ:

- What type of analysis does the newsletter use: primarily fundamental analysis, technical analysis, or a combination of both? If it uses fundamental analysis, what type of information and data does it typically focus on? If it focuses on technical analysis, what are the primary technical indicators?
- Which investment vehicles does the newsletter focus on? Does it recommend commodity stocks, futures, or exchange-traded futures? Some newsletters are even more specific. For instance, several newsletters only recommend junior gold mining stocks; others might only use options to implement their commodity strategies.
- Which markets does the newsletter focus on? Is the newsletter a generalist (recommending a variety of investments across the commodity markets), or is it specific in its focus?
- How frequent are the newsletter's recommendations? Is it a monthly newsletter? Does it offer periodic trade alerts on market-sensitive information?

- Does the newsletter make specific trade recommendations, with buy targets and stops, or does it simply recommend investments from a broader approach? For instance, if it is bullish on oil, does it recommend specific stocks or entry prices, or is it more focused on the market?

Focus on the Advisors' Backgrounds. There is no question that the newsletter advisory business is fairly lucrative. This is especially true if you have thousands of subscribers who are paying $100 a month. Some advisors open a newsletter merely for profit. They might be great marketers but poor market timers. Thus, it is important also to focus on the advisors' backgrounds. Where were they educated? What prior work experience do they have? What makes them qualified to advise investors on trades? To be sure, there is no specific style of biography that you should look for. However, you want to at least make sure that the advisors have a background in what they are writing about.

Consider the Advisors' Track Records. Part of examining advisors' backgrounds includes looking at their track records. Find out how they performed during both up and down moves in the commodity markets. Also look into whether they are consistent in their returns. A newsletter might have a substantial winner, but it might also have several more significant losses.

In some cases, you can also examine their model portfolio to see how their current recommendations are faring. The model portfolio should show the date of entry/recommendation, the current price, the percent allocation, and the percentage gain or loss. When you look at the model portfolio, remember that it might contain several dozen recommendations. It might not be realistic to hold every single position that the advisory newsletter recommends. It's also not realistic to assume that the positions you select will be the winners. Thus, make sure that you use the model portfolio more as a gauge than a predictor for how it will perform in the future.

Ask for a Free Trial and Back Issues. One of the best ways to conduct your due diligence on advisory newsletters is by asking for a free trial or back issues. Most newsletters should not have a problem with this request, and you will gain the opportunity to examine past commentary and recommendations. Look at some of the recommendations made in the past and see how they turned out. You can also get a feel for the type of analysis and commentary offered. Sometimes a newsletter might focus on markets or a style of analysis that you do not care too much about. The free trial and back issues will help you find out before you spend money and, more important, start trading.

Take Your Time. The last step that you should implement is to take your time. Do not be pressured into signing up just because they are recommending a hot company or they expect a sudden big move in certain markets. If the advisory newsletters have been around for a while, they should have no trouble finding new and consistent recommendations. So, take your time. Paper trade if you need to. When they recommend a new investment, do some of your own research. Find out if it makes sense to buy. Once you feel comfortable and have an understanding, you can use the newsletter as a form of third-party assistance.

Trading Systems

Commodity trading systems work well for technically oriented investors by providing them the opportunity to trade the commodity markets using technical analysis while systematically adhering to a set of indicators and trading rules. Trading systems are computerized models that generate buy or sell signals based on the predetermined parameters that the system is following. In other words, instead of looking at charts and using your favorite technical indicators to determine whether you should enter or exit a specific market, trading systems will trigger these signals on your behalf.

Since there are several different types of technical indicators and risk management approaches, there are also many types of commodity trading systems. Some are designed for shorter-term trades, such as day trading or scalping, and others are designed to capture longer-term trends. One thing that they all have in common, however, is that they are 100 percent systematic in their approach to the markets. Because of this systematic approach, the systems only trade technical analysis and ignore any fundamental analysis.

Pros and Cons

There are certainly pros and cons to using trading systems. The sheer fact that no fundamental analysis is used in determining whether you should enter or exit a trade leaves a fundamentally focused investor, like me, reliant solely on the mercy of the trading system. I want to make it clear that I personally don't subscribe to the theory of strictly using a trading system to manage your commodity investments. I believe that there has to be some type of fundamental approach to the markets. However, there are also some advantages to trading systems. This is especially true if you only use the systems as a form of assistance or even as a part of your overall commodity portfolio. Take a look at some of these pros and cons of trading systems.

Pros:

- *No emotion involved in trading.* When it comes to trading, one of the biggest deterrents is letting your emotions take control of the situation. This typically occurs when you say that you have a "gut feeling" that the market will rally or when you pull out your calculator and start booking the profits even before they happen. The end result of emotional trading is that investors often exit too early from a trade or stay in too long. Using a trading system often remedies the problem because you are systematically following a preset logic.
- *Disciplined approach to the markets.* Having a disciplined approach to the markets is somewhat similar to having no emotion involved in your trading. If your system enters the oil market only once it breaks out of a certain range, it will force you to adhere to that rule. With discretionary trading, it is easy to hold back from entering a trade even though your technical indicators have signaled that you should enter. This is even more significant when you have several consecutive losing trades. Normally, you might hesitate to reenter because the last trades have been awful. However, a trading system has no memory of this and simply adheres to its rules. In some

cases, that next trade could end up being the big trade for your portfolio.

- *Ability to back-test.* Given the fact that trading systems are quantitatively based, you can easily apply a certain formula and back-test how it would have performed in historical market time frames. In other words, if you know that your system will buy into a market once the 40-day moving average crosses the 80-day moving average, you can look back at the previous years and see how successful that trade would have been.

  While this will give you an idea of how successful it was in the past, by no means will it dictate how it will perform in the future. Market environments are constantly changing, and hypothetical performance is no substitute for actual performance.

- *Ability to trade a wide variety of markets.* Trading systems also allow you to trade a wide variety of markets. This makes sense since you can easily apply the same trading logic to different markets. For systems trading, the markets are all the same; it's simply a question of price movements. Conceivably, you could track and trade over 60 different markets. Without a systematic approach, there would not be enough hours in the day to monitor these markets.

- *Risk management and money management already in place.* One last advantage of trading systems is that risk management and money management are already in place. For every trade, it will always take a certain percentage risk. It will also exit a trade when it has crossed a certain threshold. And stops are typically inserted once you enter the trade.

Cons:

- *No fundamentals.* I have tracked several different trading systems in the past, and on numerous occasions a trade would occur that I would disagree with. At times I felt like screaming at the computer: Don't you know that this will occur in the next couple of days . . . or that this economic report will likely send prices the opposite way? Of course, the system has no idea and could care less. It focuses on trading the technical indicators that were part of the system. To be fair, there were times where the system was right and I was wrong. And there were also times were I was right and the system was wrong. Nonetheless, relying solely on a trading system ignores a huge part of why you are participating in the markets in the first place.

- *Will not work in all market environments.* Some trading systems simply will not work in certain environments. For instance, if your system is set up to capture long-term trends, a choppy or range-bound environment will likely result in a drawdown. The program will enter a trade when it thinks that a trend is occurring but will exit with a loss when the trend reverses. As you can imagine, if the market is choppy for a long period of time, the system will enter and exit with a loss multiple times.

> **TIP**
>
> *Focus on the fundamentals.* It is okay to look at charts and price movements, or to use technical trading strategies, but stay focused on the fundamentals and what truly drives those price movements.

Long-Term Trend-Following Systems

Long-term trend-following systems typically are set up to systematically trade various commodity markets from a trend-following perspective. The goal of trend following is that you enter a trade once it is already established, and you follow that trend until it ends. The basic idea is that you will not get in at the bottom of the trade (since the bottom would not have started), and you will not get out at the top of a trade (since the trend needs to reverse before an end to a trend is signaled). You will, however, ideally profit from the middle portion of that move. In other words, you will buy strength and sell weakness.

I believe that this type of strategy will work in the current long-term trending market environment. As I mentioned Chapter 9, one strategy is to have a long-term approach to this long-term commodities bull market. A long-term trend-following system can provide you with assistance to implement this approach.

Leveraging the Broker Relationship

The right broker can also provide you with third-party assistance. Nowadays, many investors choose to have online brokerage accounts. Nevertheless, there is a lot to be said about having an experienced broker who can assist you with trade recommendations, offer insights on the markets and economy, and answer any questions you might have. Today it is also quite convenient to find brokers who specialize in certain areas. For instance, you can find a commodity broker who focuses specifically on the agricultural markets or a stockbroker who specializes in natural resources stocks. In other words, you don't necessarily have to have one generalist broker; you can have several brokers who specialize in one or two commodity sectors.

Finding that right broker is key. In fact, when it comes to investing in this commodity bull market, finding the right broker might be one of the more important aspects. If you are content to do your own research, then this point is not as significant. However, if you are looking for additional third-party help and direction, it is important find a broker who can provide you with prudent assistance. Here are some of my thoughts about finding the right broker to help you navigate through this bull market. Find a broker who:

- Subscribes to this bull market in commodities
- Displays a certain level of expertise
- Can meet your needs
- Is reasonable in cost
- You like to talk to and likes talking to you

Subscribes to This Bull Market

You want to be able to find a broker who actually subscribes to this bull market in commodities. This can actually be much harder than you think, since the prevailing market wisdom is that we are not in a bull market. Nonetheless, it is important that your broker understands the dynamics that are affecting the commodity markets. A broker who understands why commodity prices are rising will be more likely to provide guidance and recommendations on how you can profit from this bull market. On the flip side, if your broker doesn't subscribe to the bull market, he or she will most likely try to talk you out of anything commodity related. If this is the case, why even pay him or her for advice?

A broker who believes in this bull market will also likely stay abreast of some of the factors we talked about in the first part of the book. News about increased agricultural consumption might trigger recommendations to buy specific agricultural commodities. Or the broker might be able to tell you when the commodity markets are in the midst of a sell-off or a correction.

Displays a Certain Level of Expertise

One of the hard truths about some brokers in the financial services industry is that they are simply salespeople looking to close a sale or develop a relationship with the client. In many cases, these brokers will defer to other sources for trade recommendations or information; rarely do they have the experience and knowledge to understand the commodity markets.

It is important to find a broker who has experience and is knowledgeable about the commodity markets. Ask about his or her track record or experience trading commodities. Determine what the broker is extremely knowledgeable about. If the broker is just a salesperson, find out whose recommendations he or she is making.

Can Meet Your Needs

You also want a broker who can meet your needs. If one broker is offering you a lower commission rate than another broker, this does not necessarily mean that the first broker is meeting your needs. Perhaps you are willing to pay the extra dollar amount in return for weekly market commentary, frequent trade recommendations, or simply the assurance that the broker truly knows what he or she is doing. Your broker should also offer a wide array of benefits that go beyond just simply executing your trades. Find out if there is free commentary about the markets or education on different topics. If you are looking for someone to talk with frequently, find a broker who can meet that need.

Is Reasonable in Cost

Be prepared to pay more for a broker who is acting in a full-service capacity. In other words, do not use online brokerage firms as a point of reference. It's almost comparing apples and oranges. With that said, shop around for a full-service broker who can provide the assistance that you need for a reasonable cost. It is best to ask for this commission structure early on in your interview process. Call around to a couple of different places and compare costs. Find out what the average cost is. If a broker is charging you way below average, ask how he or she is making money. If the broker is charging you three to four times the going rate, ask why. Is the broker providing you with anything else that is different from what the guy down the road would offer?

You Like to Talk to . . . and Likes Talking to You

Finally, you want to find a broker you like to talk to and who likes to talk to you. There is nothing worse than feeling rushed or that the person managing your money doesn't have time for you. Believe me, if one broker doesn't have time, someone else will. Make sure to find a broker whom you enjoy talking to and can develop a relationship with over a prolonged period of time. For instance, if you have some questions on the markets, want to talk about certain recommendations, or simply want to check on some of the broker's outlooks, you should be able to find one who will accommodate those basic needs.

Books

Books are also an excellent source of third-party help. I wrote this book to introduce you to the commodity markets on several different levels. If you want to find out more about a specific topic or subject, many specifically focused books can help you. For instance, there are books on the growth of China or of India; some books argue why we have reached a peak in oil supply; others focus on how you can use exchange-traded funds (ETFs), why you should buy gold, or the advantages of managed futures in investment portfolios. I encourage you to seek out these books for an additional layer of knowledge.

Web Sites

Web sites are by far the simplest to access, are often free, and offer abundant variety and scope. At any given hour of the day, you can get onto the Internet and view a wealth of information on trading ideas, pertinent news, contrarian commentary, or basic information on the commodity markets. Financial Web sites are a staple resource for me. I am always reading a news story, a piece of commentary, or reading an article that teaches me something new about the markets. In the same manner, I believe that many of these Web sites can offer guidance and information that will help you through various stages of this commodity bull market.

Generally speaking, the Web sites can be divided into three categories:

1. Educational
2. Content and commentary
3. News about commodity markets

In most cases, the educational Web sites do not offer opinions or perspective on the commodity markets; rather, they simply provide answers to questions that you might have about how things work or further details about the futures markets, commodity ETFs, or other investment vehicles. Some sites also provide updated supply and demand statistics on various commodities or explain different trading strategies that can be used to profit from the commodity markets.

Content and commentary Web sites also help you navigate the commodity boom. They often have up-to-date analysis about the economy, specific commodity markets, or general market trends. The nice thing about these Web sites is that you often can find different opinions on the same subject. Commentary from an author who is bullish about gold might come up next to an article by another author who feels that gold has hit its top. Additionally, the range and type of commentary on some of these sites are most likely different from what you will read in the local paper or hear from your local broker. In many cases, the opinions expressed are contrarian in nature and contain information and insights you might not have heard before.

Web sites that provide frequent news on the commodity markets or factors that affect them are also useful. For instance, these sites can help you stay abreast of the growth of the industrializing economies, the various supply and demand reports that might come out, or simply what other analysts might be saying about the markets.

My own site (www.commoditynewscenter.com) can serve as a transition from this book and also offer additional guidance for the remainder of this bull market. Here you will find:

- Current commodity news
- Commodity and economic commentary from a wide range of sources
- A blog with commentary on the happenings in the commodity markets
- Podcasts
- Quotes and charts
- Links to additional resources (books, advisory newsletters, trading systems, Web sites, etc.)
- Detailed "how-to information" about specific markets
- Forum

Conclusion

There is intrinsic value in third-party assistance. The hard part is finding the right broker, the best newsletter, or the best system that actually works. But once you do, you will have found a source that can help you siphon through a lot of information and also keep you focused on the long-term aspects of this commodity boom. Using the various third-party sources can also assist you in learning more about this commodity bull market. This book has presented you with a lot of information, but you may need to take some additional steps to put it all into action. But one thing is certain: With the knowledge you have gained, you now recognize your opportunity to take advantage of this roaring bull market in commodities.

Conclusion

Give a man a fish and he will eat for a day. Teach a man to fish and he will eat for the rest of his life.

—Chinese Proverb

The next time you order a cup of coffee, read a news story about China's growing economy, or simply turn on your air conditioner during a hot summer night, take time to consider the impact that your actions and the actions of millions of people across the globe have on the commodity markets. You should now have a much better understanding of the makeup and functions of commodity markets, the various supply and demand factors that impact commodity prices, and how prevalent this commodity bull market is in our daily lives.

Throughout this book, I have had one chief aim: to write about commodities in a simple and easy-to-understand manner that would be relevant and convincing for the average investor. I continuously asked myself: Does this point make sense to the reader who has yet to participate in the commodity markets? Does this rationale make sense to the reader who may have some misgivings about participating? I even had people who had no prior knowledge of the commodity markets read the manuscript, so I could make sure that what I was trying to communicate came across in a convincing yet clear manner.

Indeed, if some of my arguments and thoughts seem too general and broad, it was for a reason. I did not want to overwhelm you with too much technical jargon and specifics before you had a firm understanding of this commodity bull market, the different ways of participating in the markets, and the advantages that commodities can offer. This aim was extremely important when discussing a topic that is often misunderstood. In fact, this is one of the reasons why I believe some investors have not participated in the markets. They have lacked a clear understanding of how the commodity markets work.

I also wanted to write a book that was more focused on the "how" and "why" rather than the "what" and "when." In other words, I didn't want to write a book about the commodity markets that told you what to buy and when to buy it, or provide specific stock recommendations or say which markets would outperform in the next year or two. Instead, I wanted to explain the reasons why markets move the way they do and some of the steps and methods that you could implement to find the most appropriate investment for your portfolio. In short, this book should provide you with the foundational knowledge, rationale, and steps for why and how you should participate in this long-term commodity boom. Whether you take those next steps is up to you.

Real Assets. . . . Real Answers . . . Real Reasons to Participate

In closing, I want to bring up one of the more interesting conversations I have had over the last year about the transformation that is going on in China and the subsequent effects it has on commodity demand. I decided to include an interview I had with one of my clients, Yannan Shen, who recently returned to China for a college reunion. The interview sheds light on what I have stated earlier and also gives a firsthand account of the growth that has occurred in China over the last several years.

Emanuel Balarie: You recently returned to Beijing, China after 10 years. What was the biggest change that you noticed?

Yannan Shen: There are huge changes in China. A lot of places in Beijing that used to be familiar were not even recognizable. Newly constructed high-rise buildings and highways are everywhere. Beijing looks bigger than before. People's living conditions or standards are dramatically improved. One big problem is the environmental pollution; people can barely see a blue sky every day, and another problem is the water shortage throughout the northern part of China.

Emanuel Balarie: Can you elaborate on the growth of Beijing since you left?

Yannan Shen: In my old memory, there were only three beltways around metropolitan Beijing. Now Beijing has been fast growing with six perimeter highways around it. Many corporations and high-rise residential buildings have been established near the beltways. My grandparents' old house, which was located in the inner city, was torn down about three years ago, and it was replaced by a brand-new financial street with banks and investment and insurance companies from around the world. One taxi driver told me that if he stayed at home for one month, he could not even recognize some places. There are a lot of cars on the street. Taxis are everywhere, and it is very convenient to go anywhere. Traffic is always busy, and it is congested especially during the rush hour.

Emanuel Balarie: Did you have a chance to get out of the city into the country? Any noticeable changes or differences?

Yannan Shen: I did not have a chance to go to the countryside. On the way to Hang Zhou near Shanghai, we passed by a farmer's new fancy house. Some rural areas are still undeveloped, in terms of roads and public utilities.

Emanuel Balarie: Have you noticed a change in diet?

Yannan Shen: McDonald's, KFC, Pizza Hut, and Starbucks are very popular. The KFC fried chicken has been adapted with Chinese flavor, and it tastes much better than here. Children prefer to have their birthday parties in McDonald's or KFC. Milk and meat have become a big portion of people's daily diet. There are more overweight children at school than before. Also, vegetables are much fresher and less expensive than here.

Emanuel Balarie: Now, you went back for your university reunion. Since you graduated, can you tell me what (if any) changes have taken place?

Yannan Shen: We went back to the university campus and found out the old dormitories were no longer there. New dormitories were established with air-conditioners, high-speed Internet connections, and telephone. Students are enjoying better dining and study environments. After 20 years, many classmates have become experts in their fields, and a few of them even have their own business. Most of them have cars and houses.

I believe that Mrs. Shen's remarks touch on the reasons for this commodity boom. Many of my observations throughout the book are based not only on theory but on actual facts. With every McDonald's or Starbucks that is setting up shop in China, there is an increased need for industrial commodities, such as copper and oil. At the same time, these stores will not grow if there is not a certifiable need (and demand) for food commodities, such as meats and coffee. Indeed, commodity consumption will continue to intensify as industrializing economies continue to grow in terms of both infrastructure and wealth. On the supply side, there simply are not enough commodities to go around. This supply and demand imbalance is what has propelled commodity prices to decade highs and is the pivotal factor as to why prices have yet to reach their highs.

But even beyond the fundamental reasons for participating in the commodity markets, it is important to keep in mind the benefits of commodities as an asset class. Whether you want to participate in the leverage that commodity futures can offer your portfolio, whether you want to have a hedge against inflation and the declining stock market environment, or whether you simply want to add a diversifying asset to your stock and bond portfolio, allocating a portion to commodities makes sense.

References

Chapter 1

China View. "300 Million Chinese Farmers to Migrate to Cities in the Next 20 years." http://news3.xinhuanet.com/english/2006-07/30/content_4896379.htm.

Crawford, Susan. 2005. "Newly Approved Investments Expected to Strengthen Thailand's Economic and Industrial Development." *Thailand Investment Review*, Vol. 17, No. 6. www.boi.go.th:8080/issue/200507_17_6/cover.htm.

Deutsche Bank Research. *China's Commodity Hunger: Implications for Africa and Latin America*. www.dbresearch.com/PROD/DBR_INTERNET_EN-PROD/PROD0000000000199956.pdf.

Jingping, Zheng. 2005. "The Overall Economic Performance Is Good in the First Half of 2005." National Bureau of Statistics of China. www.stats.gov.cn/english/newsandcomingevents/t20050720_402264374.htm.

Mahindra World City. www.mahindraworldcity.com.

Malik, Khalid. 2004. "Sustainable Agriculture and Rural Development." United Nations Development Programme. www.undp.org.cn/print.php?sid=105.

National Center for Smart Growth Research and Education. *China Land Policy Program—Land Issues in China.* www.smartgrowth.umd.edu/chinalandpolicyprogram/landissuesinchina-tensionbetweenlandandpeople.htm.

Soneji, Haresh. 2006. "'India's Commodity Demand on the Rise.'" *Times News Network.* http://economictimes.indiatimes.com/articleshow/1826963.cms.

"The Hungry Dragon: China's Material Needs," *The Economist,* 19 February 2004 www.economist.com/business/displayStory.cfm?story_id=2446908.

Chapter 2

Candlestick Trading Forum. *The History of Japanese Candlesticks.* www.candlestickforum.com/PPF/Parameters/1_279_/candlestick.asp.

CFTC. "The Economic Purpose of the Futures Market." www.cftc.gov/opa/brochures/opaeconpurp.htm.

Chicago Board of Trade. *Our History.* www.cbot.com/cbot/pub/page/0,3181,942,00.html.

Chapter 3

Gorton, Gary B., and K. Geert Rouwenhorst. 2006, April. "Facts and Fantasies about Commodity Futures." *Financial Analysts Journal,* Vol. 62, No. 2, 47–68.

Meyer, Jack. 1996. "Despite Risks, Colleges Dabble in Commodities." *The Wall Street Journal,* November 25.

Chapter 4

Cashin P., L. Cespedes, and R. Sahay. 2003, March. "Commodity Currencies." *Finance & Development,* Vol. 40, No. 1. www.imf.org/external/pubs/ft/fandd/2003/03/cash.htm.

Chapter 5

Ahmed, Razib. 2006. "India: Coffee Consumption Increasing in Tea Drinking Country." *Indian Raj.* www.indianraj.com/2006/09/india_coffee_consumption_incre.html.

China Economic Net. "China's Copper Import Needs Outstripping Growth." http://en.ce.cn/Markets/Commodities/200604/06/t20060406_6621074.shtml.

Energy Information Administration. *World Oil Markets.* www.eia.doe.gov/oiaf/ieo/pdf/oil.pdf.

International Institute for Applied Systems Analysis. "How Did China's Grain Supply Change between 1964–1966 and 1994–1996?" www.iiasa.ac.at/Research/LUC/ChinaFood/indepth/id_4.htm.

"Life after the Oil Crash." www.lifeaftertheoilcrash.net.

Rogers, Jim. "Breakfast of Champions." www.beeland.com/Breakfast%20Cereals.htm.

The Corn and Soybean Digest. "China Still Becoming a Grain Importer." http://cornandsoybeandigest.com/ar/Brock-China-Grain-Importer-071904.

U.S. Department of Agriculture. "Cotton Consumption Higher in India Subcontinent, Lower in Turkey in 2006/2007." www.fas.usda.gov/cotton/circular/2006/06/toc.htm.

U.S. Department of Agriculture. "World Sugar Situation—2005." www.fas.usda.gov/htp/sugar/2006/World%20Sugar%20Situation%20.pdf.

U.S. Department of Agriculture Economic Research. "USDA Feeds Grain Baseline." www.ers.usda.gov/Briefing/corn/2005baseline.htm

Wang, Victor. 2006. "China's Rapid Consumption at Crossroads with Anti-Dumping Charges" *Resource Investor.* www.resourceinvestor.com/pebble.asp?relid=26959.

www.CBOT.com.

www.CME.com.

www.eia.org.

www.NYBOT.com.

www.NYMEX.com.

www.usda.gov.

Chapter 7

Idzorek, Thomas. 2006. "Strategic Asset Allocation and Commodities." *Ibbotson Associates.* www.pimco.com/LeftNav/Viewpoints/2006/Ibbotson+Commodity+Study.htm.

Chapter 10

Avery, K. 2006. *Building Wealth with Managed Futures.* Kearney, NE.: Morris Publishing, 59–60, 62–65.

Chicago Board of Trade. *Managed Futures: Portfolio Diversification Opportunities.* www.cbot.com/cbot/docs/46589.pdf.

Chicago Mercantile Exchange. *A Questions and Answer Report: Managed Futures Accounts.* http://cfisonline.com/Documents/question_and_answers_ managed_futures_accounts_CME.pdf.

CISDM Research Department. 2006. "The Benefits of Managed Futures 2006 Update." http://cisdm.som.umass.edu/research/pdffiles/benefit sofmanagedfutures.pdf.

Chapter 11

National Mining Association. "The History of Gold." www.nma.org/pdf/gold/ gold_history.pdf.

Only Gold. "The Briefest History of Gold." www.onlygold.com/TutorialPages/ HistoryFS.htm.

Smith, Adam. *Paper Money.* New York: Summit Books, 1981, 57–62.

www.worldgoldcouncil.com.

About the Author

EMANUEL BALARIE is President and Chief Investment Officer of Jabez Capital Management. Previously, Mr. Balarie was Senior Market Strategist at Wisdom Financial, Inc., and editor of *Wisdom Commodity Weekly.*

Mr. Balarie's industry experience ranges from commodity stocks to futures to alternative investments. He is a highly regarded advisor to clients and institutions on the commodity markets, and has had his research published all over the world. In addition to being a regular guest on CNBC, Balarie is frequently quoted in dozens of financial publications such as, *The Wall Street Journal*, Reuters, *Marketwatch from Dow Jones*, and *Barrons*. Mr. Balarie is a graduate of UC Berkeley.

For more information on Emanuel Balarie you can visit www.commoditynewscenter.com or email him at ebalarie@commodity newscenter.com.

Index